VILLAGES

OF

ENGLAND

VILLAGES
OF
ENGLAND

PHOTOGRAPHS BY
RICHARD TURPIN

TEXT BY
ROGER HUNT

HarperCollins*Illustrated*

First published in 1999 by
HarperCollins*Publishers*, London

Conceived and produced by
Breslich & Foss Limited
20 Wells Mews
London W1P 3FJ

Photographs © 1999 Richard Turpin
Volume copyright © 1999 Breslich & Foss Limited

ISBN 000 414 079-6

TEXT: Roger Hunt
EDITOR: Janet Ravenscroft
DESIGNER: Harry Green

JACKET PHOTOGRAPH: Upper Slaughter, Gloucestershire
TITLE PAGE PHOTOGRAPH: Frampton on Severn,
Gloucestershire

Printed and bound in Hong Kong

Contents

Introduction 6

Timber, Clay & Stone 38

The Village Green 72

The Village Church 94

Waterside Villages 124

Industrial Villages 160

Coastal Villages 188

Map and listings 210

Index 214

INTRODUCTION

Dictionaries tend to define the village as something larger than a hamlet but smaller than a town, an outline too vague to be helpful. In truth, most of us have a picture of what we imagine the village to be: it has a church, some cottages, perhaps a manor house and a village green. There is a pub and a shop; the buildings are irregular with sagging rooflines, and reflect local architectural styles. We imagine a halcyon age with quaint cottages wrapped in the sun's golden glow, an abundance of fresh produce and a carefree existence. This evocation often comes to us through literature and art that frequently ignores the harsh and gritty reality.

Once the majority of people lived in villages, but today, although there are said to be some ten thousand villages in Britain, only about a quarter of the population lives in them. The seeds for this change were sown during the seventeenth century as new agricultural practices began to transform the landscape, and were followed, from around 1760, by the far-reaching effects of the Industrial Revolution.

Although most villages have evolved gradually and grown in a fairly random fashion, some were deliberately planned. Many villages existed before the Norman conquest and were moulded by their underlying geology and location, the background of the people who lived in them, local and international politics and economics, industries and even the climate. Villages were generally sited in convenient places. Fresh water (from spring, stream or river) and dry ground were prerequisites, and a location at the junction of important track-ways or at a river crossing often caused a village to expand into a town. In some villages, cottages stretch along a single street, randomly punctuated by large houses, shops and even farm buildings. Others huddle round a green or market place and are relatively compact, whereas there are those that simply straggle into the surrounding countryside, seemingly lacking a focus. To explore a village's history, one must first untangle the web of manorial rights, parish lore, ancient field patterns and myth.

After the last Ice Age much of England was covered by forest. The first inhabitants were hunter-gatherers who travelled across wide areas in search of food and lived in temporary camps. Although man had begun clearing the forests to attract grazing animals it was not until the Neolithic period, which lasted from around 5000 to 2400 BC, that greater clearance occurred and the domestication of animals and early farming began to make a truly indelible impression on the land.

The ending of the hunter-gatherer way of life undoubtedly led to the establishment of permanent settlements. The buildings that were constructed were of wood or earth and must have been built and destroyed many times through the centuries. As they were not always rebuilt on the same site by succeeding generations, we are left with few clues as to what they were like.

Some of the villages that exist today grew up within regions defined during the Bronze and Iron Ages, but it is not until the Roman era (c.55BC–c.AD440) that a more recognisable pattern of farms, villas, towns and villages developed. However, while there is evidence of brick and stone buildings, most of the simple dwellings inhabited by ordinary people have disappeared. After the departure of the Romans in the early fifth century, central government ceased and, with the invasions of the Angles, Saxons and other Germanic peoples, a number of Roman towns collapsed, much of the countryside was drastically depopulated, and archaeology suggests that, instead of organised village communities, most early Anglo-Saxon farmsteads were isolated or in small clusters.

We have a greater understanding of late Saxon times because the Normans provided us with a vital record that reflects Britain as it was when Duke William of Normandy conquered the land and became William I of England. Although the Domesday Book of 1086 is not a record of settlements, it clearly summarises the estate pattern of the late Saxons, and provides an inventory of what the Normans took over. It paints a picture of mills, fishponds, woods, meadows and even vineyards. It tells us that there were seventy-one thousand plough teams in action, and hints at neat, self-contained villages. In reality, it is likely that England's one-and-a-half to two million inhabitants were still rather dispersed, with hamlets and farms scattered across the countryside.

Saxon lords often provided the church, or land on which one could be built, and so the boundaries of their estates became parish boundaries when these were established by the early medieval Church. When the huge estates of Saxon times were broken up after the Norman conquest, they were succeeded by manors, which effectively became autonomous administrative units under the lord of the manor to whom the majority of villagers were bound. Villages frequently grew under the protection of local landowners and manorial lords, and many of the villages we know today have their roots in this time. The feudal system, which developed in Saxon times, defined a strict social structure under which the lord had an agent, there were craftsmen who were paid for their work, and there were various levels of peasants and slaves. The Normans later clarified the system, amalgamating the peasants into one class of 'villein' and freeing the slaves. To ensure that communal activities ran smoothly, such things as the planning of the year's crops were discussed at the court of the manor, which might meet under a large oak tree on the green, or in the manor house. Here, too, disputes between neighbours were settled, and the lord enforced his rights.

Many of those components of a village that served the community as a whole were located at its centre. These included the green, the pound for stray animals, the bakehouse and the blacksmith's forge. Elsewhere in the parish there was grazing as well as

For many people, a cottage with roses round the door represents the quintessential view of the English village. This charming stone house is in the Cotswold village of Bibury in Gloucestershire.

common and wasteland. In some villages, a back lane ran parallel to the main street and formed the boundary of 'tofts': the plots of land behind the houses. These provided space in which the villagers could cultivate herbs and vegetables as well as keep poultry and perhaps a pig or cow.

Today the pub may stand in the centre of the village, but this was not an original feature. In the Middle Ages beer and ale were drunk throughout the day in preference to water, which was often

Churches, such as the church of the Holy Trinity at Bosham in West Sussex, were once central to village life. In the Middle Ages, churches were commonly the only buildings, apart from manor houses, that were built of stone.

of poor quality and liable to cause sickness. Ale was brewed at home and also drunk in private alehouses, where an ale wife, who was often a widow, brewed beer. In later years, these simple establishments often gave way to the more respectable village inn, which provided food and accommodation for visitors and travellers, and place to stable horses. The first licensing laws that regulated the sale of alcohol were not introduced until the nineteenth century.

Farming techniques varied considerably across the country. In some places, small fields enclosed by thick hedges were common; in others, there were large open fields where the three-field system was practised. In reality this had numerous variations and every generation added to and changed the pattern.

At their simplest, the three fields were arranged around the village and within these the villagers held strips of land. Each would have a share of strips spread across the fields to ensure that they had an equal proportion of good, bad and indifferent land, and a fair division of each year's rotation. The simplest form of rotation might mean that the first field contained barley, the second wheat and rye, while the third remained fallow. Instead of adopting the open-field system, some villages had an infield, which was continuously cultivated land close to the village, surrounded by an outfield where crops were rotated.

In addition, there was a meadow that provided hay for winter feed, and common pasture on which cattle or oxen could graze. These animals pulled ploughs, and supplied meat, milk and the manure that was essential fertilizer. Pigs were turned out into woodland and wasteland, which also provided wood for fuel and building material; fruits, berries and fungi for food; and reeds for roofing. Sheep, goats, ducks and geese were also kept by villagers.

In good years the land provided for the needs of all the villagers, but such subsistence farming was at the mercy of the weather. There was rarely sufficient feed to keep all the animals over the winter, which was a time of very restricted diet. People were susceptible to disease and, in times of poor harvest, the death rate went up. Plagues swept across Europe throughout the Middle Ages, but none in England was as disastrous as the Black Death of 1348–50. This disease, which is thought to have been carried into the country by rats on ships, effectively changed England for ever. It killed about a third of the population and left appalling suffering in its wake as, in many places, there were too few people to work the land. Indeed, the population didn't regain its former levels until the sixteenth century. Once-thriving communities were shattered, and some villages were abandoned. Farming methods changed as survivors shared small areas of land rather than the large fields of past times, and the feudal system slowly began to collapse. Many of the villagers who had formerly been tied to the land went instead to towns to find work. Much of the peasantry became farmers, tenant farmers and smallholders in their own right and, for some, the subsistence economy became a thing of the past. However, there remained a working class who relied on selling their labour.

At the same time, some manorial lords ceased to be farmers and became landowners with tenant farmers. In some areas large areas of open fields and commons were enclosed and put down to grass to graze sheep for the cloth industry. Many communities thrived on this industry, and the splendid 'wool' churches that were built as a result are continuing evidence of those prosperous times.

Further enclosure took place with the Dissolution of the Monasteries between 1530 and 1540, as former religious land became new estates, parks and farms. A time of considerable agrarian innovation began as new breeds of livestock, crops, farming practices and machines were adopted and perfected.

It was during the Tudor period that simple cottages became increasingly solid structures and upstairs rooms appeared. Furniture and decoration became more elaborate; gardens still served a practical purpose, but also contained flowers purely for pleasure.

The seventeenth century saw wool prices fall because of cheap imports and the increasing use of cotton and linen, but the swelling population led to a growing demand for grain and, as a result, an ever-increasing number of people faced poverty. A law of 1601 ruled that churchwardens must build housing for the poor, and a compulsory rate was imposed for the maintenance of the 'deserving' poor; however, vagabonds and beggars were treated harshly.

Throughout the late eighteenth and early nineteenth centuries, Enclosure Acts consolidated many estates. Enclosure transformed the appearance of the countryside and ended villagers' medieval rights to fish in common streams and gather wood on common land. Poaching was dealt with particularly savagely and mantraps were not made illegal until 1827.

From 1803 to 1815 the Napoleonic Wars contributed to a boom in English production of everything from wheat to cloth, but with the end of the war came a slump relieved by a brief spell of prosperity before cheap grain imports began to flood the country from America.

The slump came when village populations were still high, and to be laid off without pay meant starvation for the whole family. Even for those who had work, the wages were appallingly low, and consequently discontent grew. At the same time, mechanisation of both industrial and farm machinery caused further unemployment and threatened the livelihoods of many more people. Machinery was vandalised and, in 1830, rural unrest became so widespread throughout the south and southeastern counties that it led to rioting. The scope of the changes that took place at this time are evident in the fact that in 1851 agriculture had employed over a fifth of the population; by 1901 this had dropped to less than a tenth.

Although the First World War meant that there was again huge demand for home-grown produce, another slump followed, and by the Second World War there were thirty per cent fewer agricultural workers than there had been in 1914. In the postwar years farming increasingly involved highly efficient machinery and a considerably reduced workforce.

The pub, post office and shop are frequently a focus of village life. Here, at Great Brington in Northamptonshire, the inn bears the name Althorp, after the family estate of the late Diana, Princess of Wales, which stands nearby.

During the past fifty years huge numbers of new houses have been built in and around the old villages, many of which have become home to commuters and weekenders. Today the sons and daughters of native villagers are often unable to afford to buy property because the prices have been forced up by 'outsiders', and large supermarkets, reached by car, have greatly reduced the number of village shops. Yet many of the old community ways survive, and village fetes and a gossip on the village green remain the pleasures they have always been.

The English village is far more than just a group of buildings around a village green. Much of its essence comes from the rhythm of the seasons and its setting within the natural world of the countryside. Few understood this more than Gilbert White, who was born in the vicarage of Selborne in Hampshire on 18 July 1720. He spent virtually all his life in the village and, like his grandfather before him, became its vicar. Even when he was young he made notes on natural history and it was this interest that was to make both him and Selborne famous. His classic book, *The Natural History and Antiquities of Selborne*, was published in 1788. It had its origins in *White's Garden Kalendar*, begun in 1751, in which he recorded both the work done in the garden of his house, 'The Wakes', and notes on such things as how the house martin builds its nest. 🦋

A bove the village of Selborne lies an area of woodland called the Hanger, and one would like to think that the view from there has changed little since the days of Gilbert White. The village clusters around a green that was formerly a market place. Almost opposite this is White's home, which was a private house until the last owner died in 1953. Subsequently it was turned into a museum that contains not only a collection relating to Gilbert White and Selborne, but also exhibits associated with the Oates family. Captain Lawrence Oates accompanied Captain Robert Falcon Scott to the South Pole in 1912, but died, along with his four companions, on the return journey.

The Reverend Gilbert White is buried in the churchyard of the church of St Mary, where his memorial window depicts St Francis feeding the birds. ❧

The village of Selworthy was created in 1828 by Sir Thomas Acland on his Holnicote estate in west Somerset. Acland took a keen interest in religion, education and the well-being of his workers, and the cottages were built to house his retired servants. Grouped around a sloping green, the cottages mirror the vernacular architecture of the much older buildings in neighbouring villages. To enhance his 'happy valley', Acland planted trees on the surrounding hillsides and encouraged his tenants to dress in red cloaks on Sundays.

Near the cottages there is a medieval stone tithe-barn and standing above the village is the mainly fourteenth-century church of All Saints, which is notable for its lavish interior, especially the fine wagon roof that spans the south aisle. In 1944 Selworthy was given to the National Trust, and it now lies within the Exmoor National Park. ❧

Originally known as 'direction posts' or 'direction stones', signposts were first required by law in 1697 when travel along England's roads was increasing. They tended to be erected rather haphazardly, and it was not until the time of the turnpike acts of the eighteenth century that the provision of direction posts became compulsory at turnpike crossroads. Such signs were often placed higher than normal finger posts so that the writing on them could be read easily by the stagecoach driver.

Signs have served many other purposes through the history of the village. House-numbering was once unknown, so traders distinguished themselves by their signs: the barber's pole, the pawnbroker's three balls and the chemist's pestle and mortar are some that survive today. Such signs were suspended over the footpath by iron or wooden attachments and there was a constant danger that they might fall. With the advent of house-numbering, most hanging signs were abolished in 1762. ❧

Agriculture has had a dramatic effect on the landscape. Nowhere is this more true than on the edges of the North Yorkshire moors. Athough the vast expanse of heather-covered moors may appear to be an unspoilt wilderness, the moors were created by Bronze Age settlers who cleared the forests and introduced cattle, which prevented regeneration. Today's farming patterns are superimposed on this earlier land use, with isolated farm buildings adding to the charm of the landscape.

Lying below the Cleveland Hills, just within the northwest edge of the North York Moors National Park, Carlton-in-Cleveland developed in Saxon times, and jet has been mined in the area since the Middle Ages. The jet industry and the extraction of alum – a mineral used in the manufacture of cloth, tanning and medicine – led to a steady stream of packhorse trains passing through the district.

Through the village, between grassy banks, runs Alum Beck, which is crossed by a ford and a number of bridges. The present church of St Botolph was not built until 1896, although an earlier church had been built by a Reverend George Sanger. When the Reverend Sanger first arrived in the village, he found the church derelict and set about building a new one. As well as raising the funds, he did the labouring himself, and finally completed the church in 1881. It was soon destroyed by fire and Sanger was charged with arson, but subsequently was acquitted.

The church of St Mary stands at the centre of the village of Lasting-ham, with the wide expanse of the North York Moors National Park stretching to the horizon beyond. In AD 654 a monastery was founded here by St Cedd, a monk from Lindisfarne or Holy Island off the coast of Northumberland. The monastery was struck by plague, and Cedd was amongst those who died. However, after his death, his youngest brother, Chad, established a community that survived for two centuries before being destroyed by the Danes in 866. The monastery was re-founded in 1078, but abandoned before 1086. The crypt, however, survives and is thought to stand over the grave of St Cedd.

In the eighth century the Venerable Bede described Lastingham as 'among steep and solitary hills, where you would rather look for the hiding places of robbers and the lairs of wild animals than the abodes of man'. Tastes have changed, however, and on a clear day, views over the moors are breathtaking and, in the spring, pockets of woodland are suf-fused with the heady scent of bluebells. 🪷

Lying close to the coast, on the edge of the Quantock hills in Somerset, the village of East Quantoxhead is claimed to be the only piece of land in the county to have remained unsold since the time of the Conquest, when the area was parcelled out to Norman barons. The Luttrell family, who have owned the village for centuries, are remembered in the small church of St Mary where the tomb of Hugh Luttrell has stood since he died in 1522. In the porch is an interesting example of a coffin squint, a small aperture in the wall from which the waiting priest can watch the funeral cortège approach.

The family also built nearby Dunster Castle, now in the care of the National Trust. The castle's thirteenth-century gatehouse survives but the building itself was remodelled between 1868 and 1872 by Antony Salvin, an authority on the restoration and improvement of castles. ❧

Luccombe cottages are mainly colour-washed and built of 'cob', a mixture of earth and straw. Some cob buildings are known to date from the fifteenth century. The West Country saying, 'all cob wants is a good hat and a good pair of shoes', refers to the practice of building on a plinth of stone and topping the structure with a roof of thatch. In recent years there has been a considerable revival of interest in traditional building methods, such as cob, because they use readily available, natural materials and thus have a limited impact on the environment. ❧

Lying on a hill at the heart of the South Downs, the village of Amberley in West Sussex displays a great variety of house and cottage styles and a diversity of building materials that includes flint, brick and timber. The village overlooks the River Arun, which frequently floods the large tract of land to the north known as the Wildbrooks. A railway was built across this area in 1863 and was considered to be a great feat of engineering.

At the edge of the village, next to the Norman church of St Michael, are the ruins of Amberley Castle, which must once have guarded the gap where the Arun breaks through the chalk of the Downs. Originally it was a manor house that served as a retreat for the bishops of Chichester. In 1388 the bishop's records show that there were thirty-six acres of meadowland, and that ninety-two acres of parish land were sown with crops, including wheat, barley, beans and peas. ❧

Steeply gabled roofs and grey stone are punctuated by lush gardens at the hilltop village of Bisley in Gloucestershire. This was once a textile village, and many of the cottages were occupied by weavers who operated their hand looms at home.

Nearby is the medieval Over Court, which was granted to Elizabeth I as part of her estate before she became queen. She is said to have stayed at the house as a child and, many years later, workmen digging nearby came upon a medieval coffin containing the bones of a young girl. From this a legend grew up that Elizabeth had died during her visit and that the coffin contained her remains. It was said that the villagers, fearing the wrath of Henry VIII, decided to send a substitute back to Court, but that the only child with a likeness to Elizabeth was a boy, and so it was that the 'Bisley Boy' reigned as Queen of England. ❧

In 1809, Jane Austen moved to a modest two-storey brick house, now a museum, in the village of Chawton in Hampshire. The house was on the Chawton House estate, which belonged to Jane's brother, Edward. Jane shared the house with her mother, her sister Cassandra and a family friend, Martha Lloyd. They kept a maid and a man for outdoor work, but did much to run the house and tend the garden themselves. Jane either walked or used a donkey cart to reach the nearby market town of Alton to the north. The unmarried daughter of a clergyman, she completed six novels, three of which are known to have been written in the family parlour at Chawton. ❦

Lying in comparatively remote countryside near the upper reaches of the River Thames in Oxfordshire, Kelmscott is still essentially rural. The village is quite spread out, with the church at one end and the manor house, in which the artist William Morris lived, at the other. The painter and poet Dante Gabriel Rossetti described Kelmscott as 'the doziest dump of old grey beehives', but in sunlight the stone that is everywhere in the village takes on a warm glow.

One of Morris's many achievements was the founding, in 1877, of the Society for the Protection of Ancient Buildings (SPAB) to counteract the often destructive 'restoration' of medieval buildings then being practised by Victorian architects. The SPAB is still active today, and a large number of the old buildings that stand in the villages of England owe their architectural integrity to Morris's foresight and the ongoing work of the Society. ❦

The Memorial Cottages at Kelmscott were built in 1902 by William Morris's wife, Jane, as a memorial to him. The relief on the front of the cottages depicts Morris with his hat, satchel and stick beside him, and farm buildings in the background. When Morris died, the doctor wrote that: 'the disease is simply being William Morris, and having done more work than ten men'. Morris was indeed hugely energetic: as well as being a poet, he was foremost in inspiring the Arts and Crafts movement. As a craftsman he resisted the mass-production of the Victorian age and founded the famous Morris and Co., for whom he designed furniture, wallpapers and textiles. Many of his designs remain influential today. Morris was also involved in printing and typography. After visiting Iceland, he translated Icelandic sagas, and later also wrote several historical romances. Although he came from a solid middle-class background, he eventually became a committed socialist and was one of the founding fathers of the British socialist movement. ॐ

Built of local stone and partly hidden by its garden wall, Kelmscott Manor is Elizabethan with seventeenth-century additions. It was William Morris's country home for twenty-five years. He came to live there in the summer of 1871, sharing the rent with his former friend and wife's lover Dante Gabriel Rossetti. While Rossetti hated the discomforts and cold of the house, Morris appreciated the magic and beauty of the manor and its setting. However, Morris avoided the house while Rossetti was there, and it was not until after the joint tenancy ended in 1874 that he began to stay there more often. With its simple vernacular style, the manor is typical of so many of the buildings Morris sought to save. Later, when he started his own printing works at his west London home in Hammersmith, he called the company Kelmscott Press. ❧

Gardens such as these at Selborne in Hampshire play a significant role in giving each village its character. In the Middle Ages, gardens were simply places in which to grow vegetables and fruits for the table. Herbs were grown by the religious orders and dispensed as medicines but, after the Dissolution of the Monasteries, villagers would have had to cultivate their own. No one knows when flowers were first planted around cottages purely for pleasure, but it is likely that the styles employed by the wealthier classes in Elizabethan times were copied by villagers who probably collected plants and seeds from the wild.

TIMBER, CLAY & STONE

ALBURY, SURREY • BAINBRIDGE, NORTH YORKSHIRE • BLAKENEY, NORFOLK
BROADWAY, HEREFORD AND WORCESTER • CHALFORD, GLOUCESTERSHIRE
CLARE, SUFFOLK • CROSBY GARRETT, CUMBRIA
FRAMPTON ON SEVERN, GLOUCESTERSHIRE • GREAT TEW, OXFORDSHIRE
HARTINGTON, DERBYSHIRE • HAWORTH, WEST YORKSHIRE • HORRINGER, SUFFOLK
LAVENHAM, SUFFOLK • LUXULYAN, CORNWALL • OCKHAM, SURREY • SMARDEN, KENT
ST JOHN'S BECK, CUMBRIA • STANTON, GLOUCESTERSHIRE • TONG, SHROPSHIRE
TURTON, LANCASHIRE • UPPER SLAUGHTER, GLOUCESTERSHIRE
WEOBLEY, HEREFORD AND WORCESTER • WHALLEY, LANCASHIRE • WITLEY, SURREY

COTTAGES, MANOR HOUSES, CHURCHES AND MILLS form the essence of a village and, through their architecture and use of building materials, give us a distinct sense of their own particular area of England. Traditionally, people built their homes with the materials that were closest to hand, so a rich diversity of building styles developed across the country. It was only with the coming of the canals, and later the railways, that transportation of materials from one region to another became relatively easy and inexpensive. Even then it was often only in the towns and cities that these 'imported' materials were used.

Timber was the preferred building material for centuries, yet today the distribution of timber structures does not reflect its former importance in virtually all areas of England. Few buildings have escaped alteration or extension, and frequently the original structure is hidden behind 'skins' of external cladding or finishes intended to protect it from the elements or adapt it to suit changing fashions.

Various forms of construction are used in timber-framed buildings, the most basic of which is the 'cruck'. The crucks were pairs of tree trunks set into the ground and fixed at the top to form a framework that has a distinctive triangular appearance. Other timber buildings are constructed so that the entire roof weight is supported on the wall frames.

Oak is the traditional wood used in timber-framed buildings. It was generally 'green' or freshly felled, so relatively unseasoned, but it has proved durable and strong. The frames themselves, which were prefabricated on the ground, were secured at the joints by oak pegs. 'Carpenters' marks' – a modified form of Roman numerals – were scribed on the timbers to ensure that they could be re-assembled correctly on site. The gaps in the frame were filled with wattle and daub – a lattice panel of hazel or willow covered in a mixture of clay, dung and straw – or, later, by a framework of lath and plaster, or brick.

Timber-framing is not always evident because many frames were plastered over. Sometimes the plaster was indented or moulded to form patterns or ornate detail known as 'pargetting', which was at its most popular in the second half of the seventeenth century in Essex, Suffolk and southeast England.

Despite its charm, wood was generally regarded as inferior and, in many otherwise timber-framed villages, the more prestigious buildings were stone: most notably the church and the manor house. Surprisingly perhaps, stone is not as ancient a building material as we might imagine. The Saxons used stone, as is still evident in the surviving parts of many churches, but when William I defeated King Harold at the Battle of Hastings in 1066, stone houses were rare.

However, during the Middle Ages stone became a much more common building material especially across the great swathes of country where it was easy to find. The way stone walls were built depended on the type of stone available, local tradition, the quality of the building and period preferences. Cottage walls were often constructed of rubble or unfinished stones that were sometimes squared and laid in courses. The walls of better houses were built with ashlar: blocks of dressed stone laid in even courses with almost invisible mortar joints between them. It is not just houses that reflect the qualities of the local stone: it can also be seen in the walls that divide fields, and the headstones in the local churchyard.

Running almost 50 miles (80 kilometres) mainly through the county of Gloucestershire, the Cotswold hills have provided ample building material for centuries. Limestone predominates in this landscape, and abandoned quarries abound. Because it is fairly easy to work, limestone was refined to form architectural detail such as

This door knocker at the twelfth-century Turton Tower in Lancashire is typical of many small architectural details that survive. Such items enhance England's buildings and demonstrate the considerable skills of the blacksmith and other village craftsmen.

the moulded mullions of windows, and flourishes such as carvings and finials. Limestone is found in other parts of the southwest, Oxfordshire, Northamptonshire, parts of Lincolnshire and North Yorkshire, but, like all types of stone, its local character depends on how it was wrought and tempered by nature.

Sandstone is common in the old industrial towns of Yorkshire and northern England, although the grimy, lifeless, soot-laden buildings with which it is all too often associated do it little justice. Sandstone buildings tend to have a certain ruggedness because it is not an easy stone to decorate. Softer sandstone crumbles and loses its detail; harder types are simply too difficult to work. Typical is millstone grit, a tough and gritty sandstone which, as its name suggests, was used to make millstones. Originally quarried by the Romans, it later became the principal building stone of the southern Pennines.

In the south and southeast of England, flint gives a dark, lustrous quality to many village buildings. To provide a flat outer surface to a wall, the egg-shaped flints were split or 'knapped'. In other places, cobbles and pebbles gathered from the seashore, riverbeds or local fields were used, and were often rendered or even tarred.

Bricks are such a common building material right across the country that we barely notice them. However, their colour, texture and size, the way they are laid and the mortar used to bond them all play a part in creating the character of the English village. It was the Romans who brought the art of brick-making to Britain. The skill was revived in the Middle Ages and spread across the eastern, clay-bearing regions, the mid-lands and the north. In Tudor times brick-making was perfected and bricks became a prestigious alternative to stone, but by the middle of the seventeenth century bricks were as cheap as timber.

Two main ingredients give clay its wide range of colours: iron and free lime. Iron is the source of the reds, blues and darker colours produced by the hard northern clays, while free lime bleaches out most colours to give the buff, softer, more absorbent southern varieties. Handmade bricks varied considerably in size, shape and quality. The high water content of the clay caused varying amounts of shrinkage as they were fired, and colour differences occurred as the heat affected exposed surfaces far more than those in contact with other bricks.

Early bricks were generally longer, wider and shallower than modern ones, and different colours went in and out of fashion as tastes changed. Bricks were frequently made on site from local clay, so regional variations developed. Patterns, or bonds, with names such as English Garden Wall, English Cross and Flemish Garden Wall were created by overlapping bricks. These patterns gave walls both strength and symmetry.

Some walls that appear to be of brick are, in fact, clad with what are known as mathematical tiles. These were designed to imitate bricks and were hung from timber boarding or laths. Their joints were pointed in mortar, just like bricks, and to maintain the illusion, specially shaped tiles were sometimes used at corners. Found mainly in the southeast, they became fashionable towards the middle of the eighteenth century, but were used well into the nineteenth century.

Tile cladding was also common in the southeast and was often used on timber-framed buildings. Ordinary clay roofing tiles were generally used, but some were specially made with a shaped bottom edge for decorative effect and, by using a variety of colours, patterns were sometimes created. Slate tiles were used in a similar way in other parts of the country.

Earth – variously termed cob, mud, wichert, pisé and clay lump – is an ancient walling material that was frequently used for cottages and smaller farm buildings in Devon, Corn-

wall and East Anglia. Cob generally contained clay soil, chalk, chopped straw and gravel and was gradually built up in layers, which meant that it could take two years to build a two-storey house. Clay lump was shaped into blocks with moulds and left to dry before use. Such buildings were protected from the elements by a skin of lime render, and were then coated with limewash.

The material used to build this simple stone bellcote at the village of Upper Slaughter in Gloucestershire was probably taken from one of the numerous quarries that once existed in the parish.

Surviving cob buildings often retain their thatched roofs. Until the end of medieval times, thatch was the most common form of roof covering, but there are distinct regional variations. In the West Country, roofs are generally simple and have a gentle pitch and soft curves, while in the eastern counties, pitches are steeper and the appearance of the thatch is more angular and often decorative.

Ramshackle sheds and lopsided agricultural buildings contribute their own charm to a village, but it is the timber-framed buildings with their silvery oak, the earthen hues of limewashed cottages or the panoply of stone and brick houses that most often capture the imagination.

To many people, Broadway in Worcester-shire is the quintessential Cotswolds village. It boasts a range of buildings from many periods, but the stone with which they are built has been used with such care that it displays its texture, shape and colour to best advantage. It was only towards the end of the nineteenth century that people began to visit the Cotswolds to admire the distinctive vernacular architecture, and Broadway became a favourite place for artists and intellectuals.

Some of the buildings along the High Street have bay windows on the ground floor which, in many cases, were probably added early in the nineteenth century to accommodate shop fronts. The Lygon Arms hotel is one of the most notable buildings in the village. Once called the White Hart, it was originally a private manor house. The date 1620 is carved on a door surround, and there is a chimneypiece that may date from the time of Henry VIII.

The village lies close to the base of Fish Hill, which rises to over 1,000 feet (300 metres). At its peak is the distinctive landmark of Broadway Tower, a folly that was built in 1800 by the Earl of Coventry. The tower could be seen from the earl's family seat some 20 miles (32 kilometres) away at Worcester. ❧

Lying on the level clay plain of the Kentish Weald, Smarden owed its prosperity to the wool trade. It was licensed as a market town by Edward III in 1332, but it never grew larger than a village.

Smarden has a wealth of timber houses, and it was in the central Weald that the so-called Wealden house evolved. Occupied by yeoman farmers, such houses had an almost standard plan based on a simple rectangle with a hipped roof. At the centre was an open hall two storeys high, while at one end was the parlour with a room for sleeping above. At the other end was a pantry and buttery, again with a store room or sleeping room above. The upper rooms were jettied, projecting out over the walls of the ground floor. However, the most characteristic feature of the Wealden house is generally the fact that the area above the hall itself is not jettied, so the eaves of this part of the roof are supported by large curved timber brackets. ❦

The oldest gravestones in the churchyard of St Michael's at Smarden date from the late seventeenth century, when classes other than the gentry began to commemorate their dead. They are every bit as important to the architecture of the village as the buildings and, in stone-bearing areas, they frequently reflect the underlying geology. The best of them are a tribute both to the dead and to the skill of the long-forgotten masons who crafted the stones.

This farmhouse and cottage at Great Tew in Oxfordshire are built with the honey-coloured limestone that is typical of the area. The village is in perfect harmony with the landscape, an effect that is not entirely due to accident. In the early nineteenth century changes were made so that the village could be seen from the estate, and blend with it in a pleasing way. At that time the estate was managed by one John Claudius Louden, who both practised and wrote about gardening and architecture. He was just twenty-six when he arrived, and soon set about creating an experimental farm and making improvements to the estate, the surrounding landscape and buildings in the village.

In the seventeenth century Great Tew had been the home of Lord Falkland, who invited writers and scholars such as Ben Johnson and Edmund Waller to his home. Sadly, the original house was destroyed by fire and all that remains today are the garden walls. ❧

avenham in Suffolk has often been described as England's most perfect medieval village because it is rich in buildings of the period. The timber framing has mellowed to silver, the plasterwork is of every earthen hue and all is topped by roofs of undulating clay tiles. Such buildings have a softness of appearance derived from the totally natural quality of the materials used. The spaces between the

close-grained oak timbers were filled with wattle and daub, plastered with a lime render, then finished with a protective coating of lime-wash built up over time by regular application.

Lime is made by burning chalk or limestone, then 'slaking' the resulting quicklime with water to make a putty, which in turn is mixed with sand to produce mortar or render. Limewash is made with putty lime to which pigments can be added. At quiet times of the year, farm labourers often set to work applying limewash to village buildings. Before about 1850, most buildings were built and maintained with lime.

In 1536 the abbot of Whalley Abbey and his monks joined the Pilgrimage of Grace, during which England's northern counties revolted against religious and economic changes. As a consequence, the abbot and his followers were convicted of high treason and the abbot was hanged outside the fourteenth-century abbey gatehouse (left).

Early doors, such as this one at Whalley Abbey, were constructed of heavy vertical planks and were often of oak. These planks were fixed to horizontal rails or another layer of planks, and are studded with the ends of wooden or iron pegs. Medieval doors frequently did not have frames, so their large wrought-iron hinges were attached directly to the stone wall on iron brackets that were built into the door jamb. These doors were often secured with a heavy drawbar. In time, the pointed medieval door became round headed and, during the seventeenth century, this gave way to the flat-topped classical panelled door associated with the Georgian era.

The parish of Chalford near Stroud in Gloucestershire was created during the twelfth century. Today its collection of stone houses forms a picturesque scene, but the village had its heyday in the nineteenth century when it was semi-industrialised. Not far from the wealthy clothiers' fine houses are the cottages in which spinners and weavers lived and worked. These workers paid between £6 and £9 a year in rent at a time when the average weekly wage was about ten shillings, and most of this went on food. As a result, poverty was widespread.

During the period between 1790 and 1825 some two hundred mills and associated buildings were built in the south Cotswolds to serve the cloth industry. In 1783 work on the Thames and Severn Canal began, and within six years it was the first inland waterway to link the two rivers. The canal had a short life, partly due to problems with the water level caused by its porous limestone bed, but the section from Chalford to Stroud continued to serve local trade throughout the nineteenth century, and a canal maintenance man's stone roundhouse of around 1790 survives. ❧

Windows are so much a part of virtually every building that it is easy to take them for granted. The window openings of early timber-framed buildings were formed as part of the frame itself. These were often divided by wooden mullions, and wooden shutters, oiled cloth or paper were used to reduce draughts. When glass became more readily available in the sixteenth century, window frames were adapted to accept small square or diamond-shaped panes or 'quarries' of glass set in thin strips of lead known as 'cames', as at the church of St Mary at Whalley (left). Glass like this was made using processes that created slight blemishes. This, and the fact that each pane of glass is held at a slightly different angle causes the window to sparkle and flash in the light. ❧

Tile-hung buildings abound in Kent, Sussex and Surrey where, in villages such as Witley (above), they add a warm richness to the scene. First appearing towards the end of the seventeenth century, the original purpose of tile-hanging, or weather-tiling as it is sometimes known, was to provide protection for timber-framed buildings. Generally, the tiles covered the upper storeys only but, in a few cases, they were taken right to the ground. Plain clay roofing tiles were most commonly used, although tiles with a shaped bottom edge were employed for decorative effect. Sometimes patterns were created by using tiles of different colours or by hanging courses of alternating plain and patterned tiles. ❧

Thatching and topiary are two ancient arts that have been brought together at this cottage in Horringer in Suffolk to form an interesting pattern of straight lines and curves. Topiary has been practised since Roman times, but became particularly fashionable in England in the sixteenth century. The Victorians considered it vulgar and topiary fell out of fashion, but today one still sees small cottage gardens that are entirely dwarfed by giant birds and figures.

Thatch is just as attractive as topiary, but has a far more practical purpose and has undergone something of a revival in recent years. The thatcher can cultivate his own individual style around gables and dormers and along ridges, but there are also distinct regional variations that have often been passed down through thatching families. Before the coming of the combine harvester and the cultivation of shorter-stemmed wheat in the 1950s, the most common material used for thatching was wheat straw. When the supply of this became limited, many thatchers had to learn the technique of thatching in reed. ❧

The nature of the village house has changed greatly over the centuries. Once, only important buildings like the church and the manor house were built of anything other than timber. Most cottages were simple and not particularly well built, but they offered the villager a place to eat and sleep, and perhaps carry on a craft that would help to pay the rent. Family life and work were inextricably linked, and there was little thought or effort given to the external appearance of such homes. In time, the more prosperous farmers and merchants started to follow the styles of the day and to build properties of substance, such as this house in Frampton on Severn in Gloucestershire (left). The use of materials such as brick became fashionable and these homes are now often highly sought after.

An abundance of timber-framed houses survives in the village of Weobley in Herefordshire. In this photograph (above), 'cruck' framing can clearly be seen at the end of a building that was once part of an old barn. Large trees with a natural curve were used to form buildings of this type. The timbers were either taken whole or cut into two matching halves to achieve symmetry. Before the Middle Ages, these 'blades' would have been sunk straight into the earth, but later they were mounted on a beam resting on a low stone plinth. They were then joined together where they met at the apex of the roof, and the same arrangement was repeated at intervals along the length of the building, creating what are known as 'bays' in between. At first such houses probably only had one floor, but horizontal beams were introduced later to span the distance between the crucks and support an upper storey. Cruck-framed buildings are found in most parts of the north, southwest and midlands of England, but are surprisingly absent in the eastern and south-eastern lowlands, where other forms of timber framing do, nonetheless, exist.

Lying in the Peak District of Derbyshire, above Beresford Dale and the River Dove, the village of Hartington is now a tranquil place, but the surrounding countryside was once mined and quarried for lead and stone. North of here, beneath a covering of heather and peat, the local stone is a type of sandstone called mill-stone grit. The landscape around Hartington is softer and greener because this is limestone country. However, the tower of the late-thirteenth-century church of St Giles that rises above the cottages and the market place is built of red ashlar sandstone. Sandstone was used for the church for the simple reason that limestone rarely provides the cleanly squared blocks necessary for this type of building. However, it is suitable for rubble walling, so it was used in the drystone field walls as well as in the construction of the older houses in the village. ❧

Field boundaries are defined in a variety of ways across England, depending largely on the availability of materials. Around St John's Beck in Cumbria (right) drystone walling is the most common method. Since no mortar is used, each stone is held in place by weight, friction and the skill of the builder. The interlocking construction means that even if the land beneath shifts, the wall can move without collapsing. Drystone walling is an ancient craft that has hardly changed over the centuries, but the skill of the 'waller' was firmly established when enclosure acts led to the construction of thousands of miles of walls in the eighteenth and nineteenth centuries. Most of the walls standing today have their origins in that period. ❧

The pattern of the landscape around Bainbridge in North Yorkshire is punctuated by field barns, of which there are said to be some ten thousand dotted across the Pennines. With low pitched roofs and walls that have projecting 'throughstones', they are built from the local limestone and combine a shelter for livestock on the ground floor with a hay store in the loft above. In Anglo-Saxon England, barley was the principal crop, and the word barn is derived from the Old English 'bern' or 'bereærn', meaning barley house. Their construction varies depending on their location: barns in the south and southeast of England are generally timber framed and weather boarded with a thatched or tiled roof. ❧

The plaster decoration on this fifteenth-century priest's house in Clare, Suffolk (left), is called pargetting. The art of decorative exterior plasterwork was commonly practised in the seventeenth century and is most often found in southeast England, particularly in Suffolk and Essex. Pointed sticks, which were sometimes tied together to make a fan or comb, were used to produce simple incised patterns in damp lime plaster. More complex relief designs, such as the ones shown, required far greater skill and they would have been either cast or built up layer by layer using wet plaster.

The church of St Andrew stands on a steep hill overlooking the fells around the Cumbrian village of Crosby Garrett. Local tradition has it that, when the devil saw stones at the bottom of the hill lying ready to build the church, he put them in his apron and carried them to the top.

There are numerous signs of early human habitation in the surrounding countryside. In the nineteenth century a number of cairns on both Irton Hill and Bents Hill were excavated and human bones were found within. A cairn at Rayseat Pike was excavated and found to contain cremated remains. Beneath it was a large standing stone measuring some 6 feet (1.8 metres) in height. An iron knife, shears, buckle and a bridle bit were discovered at another nearby site.

Wrapped in the blooms of a long-established wisteria, this house at Ockham in Surrey has the satisfied look of age. At first sight its façade reveals little, but there are signs of changes in the building's history. Few village houses were designed by architects and many properties underwent considerable changes as they were adapted to suit the fashions of the period and the needs of those who owned them. Many houses have grown from compact dwellings to much larger, rambling homes with an appearance very different from the original. In Georgian times considerable numbers of timber-framed houses were re-fronted in brick, while others have been hidden behind a screen of tile-hanging or mathematical tiles.

Often the most obvious signs of change are clearly visible from the exterior of a house: the windows may seem unbalanced or may be of markedly different styles and patterns; there may even be a mixture of casements and sashes. Frequently the roofline varies and so too does the detailing of the brick courses and other embellishment.

The area around Albury in Surrey is scattered with small cottages, many of which are tile-hung like the one shown in the picture below. The village of Albury originally stood close to the mansion of Albury Park, but today all that is left there is the Saxon church of St Peter and St Paul and a few scattered cottages. Around 1780 the villagers were forced to move when the owner of the estate closed the roads through the park, enclosed the village green and annexed a corner of the churchyard to form part of his grounds. The majority of the villagers moved to Weston Street, a hamlet a short distance to the west, which has become the present village of Albury. To accommodate the additional population the estate constructed cottages, and a new brick church of St Peter and St Paul was erected there in 1842. The original Tudor mansion of Albury Park was destroyed by fire in 1697, and a new house was built on the site. A later owner engaged the architect Augustus Pugin, who remodelled the house and added sixty-three ornate brick chimneys.

The architect Sir Philip Stott bought the estate at Stanton, in Gloucestershire, in 1906 and lived there until his death in 1937. Employing skilled craftsmen, his sympathetic restoration ensured that the village and its buildings have survived remarkably well. Standing at the foot of Shenberrow hill, the village has a medieval cross and a seventeenth-century sundial and globe while, on either side of the main street, there are gabled houses and cottages built around 1600.

The derivation of the village name is 'farm on stony ground', and the Cotswold stone used there probably came from the once-prolific quarry above the village. Large estates frequently had their own quarries; the villagers had the right to dig stone from quarries found on common land. On hillsides, stone was mined rather than quarried since it was far easier to reach the best beds by tunnelling rather than digging from above through large quantities of unsuitable material. Although seemingly the same throughout the area, such stone varies quite considerably from quarry to quarry in its quality, texture and colour. ❧

Granite dominates the view from the churchyard at Luxulyan in Cornwall (right). The church of St Ciricius and St Julitta is itself built from large blocks of local granite and dates mainly from the fifteenth century. Quarrying granite was uneconomic until the nineteenth century, so the stones used were those found on the moors. In the countryside this moorstone was used to construct bridges and gate posts. Before the introduction of mechanical cutting techniques, cottages were built using the largest stones at the bottom and the smaller, lighter ones higher up. Because the stones were often of differing sizes, they were not always laid in regular courses, but the squarest blocks were reserved for the corners. Cornish granite can be seen in many other areas of the country because, as well as being exceptionally hard, it is generally impervious to water. As a result it has been used extensively to build such things as docks and breakwaters. In the nineteenth century it was used for paving, and granite blocks were laid in streets across the country. ❧

The chalk deposits found in the southern and eastern counties of England yield an abundant supply of flint. At Blakeney in Norfolk the grey hue of the rounded stones is set off by the warm appearance of brick dressings. Almost pure silica, flint is an incredibly hard material and resists the elements extremely well. It can also be broken or 'knapped', and was frequently laid with the broken surface outwards, which gives the wall a black lustrous quality. The shape of flint makes it difficult to lay and in order to create square corners, such as at the junctions of windows and doors, it is generally reinforced with other materials. Flint was sometimes used with limestone or brick to form patterns, often to spectacular effect. ❧

Lying in England's industrial north, the Yorkshire village of Haworth has rugged moorland to the west and the town of Bradford to the east. Millstone grit was used here before the Norman conquest, and the coarse gritty sandstone dominates the surrounding country-side. The stone is often brownish-yellow, but in the villages many of the buildings have weath-ered to black. The weather here can be severe, and trees are scarce on the high moors, having either been felled for fuel or stunted by past industrial pollution. This uncompromising landscape did, however, serve as inspiration to the Brontë sisters, and is brought vividly to life in Emily's *Wuthering Heights*.

The underlying stone has been quarried not just for buildings and roof tiles, but for paving and millstones, and was used in the construction of great town halls and churches. 🕊

Porches were developed for the practical purpose of reducing draughts and protecting the door from the elements, but they became increasingly ornate. Houses, such as this one at Tong in Shropshire, were given a delicate elegance by the ironwork of their trellis-type porches. Cast iron, which is an alloy of iron and carbon, was not used for any significant architectural work until 1714 when cast-iron railings were erected around St Paul's Cathedral in London. Early cast items were relatively coarse but, by the end of the Georgian era, casting techniques had improved to such an extent that cast iron became the preferred material for decorative work. Ambitious schemes became possible at a lower cost because designs could be taken from pattern books and items were available ready-made. In buildings of the Regency period iron made a considerable architectural contribution and was used extensively in creating ornate verandas, fanlights and staircase balustrades. 𓆸

Pronounced 'Lucksillian', the village of Luxulyan in Cornwall has given its name to 'luxulianite', a porphyritic granite that can be seen around the area as enormous isolated blocks. Some 6 miles (10 kilometres) away lies the wild expanse of Bodmin moor, where primitive people built dwellings and attempted to clear the granite moorstones so that they could cultivate the land. Centuries later, the community was engaged in quarrying china clay or kaolin, a valuable mineral that brought a profitable industry to the area.

The name of the village probably has Celtic origins and means 'Sulian's monastery'. In the Middle Ages the chapel of St Sulian was a shrine on the route between St Benet's Abbey at Lanivet and Tywardreath Priory near St Blazey. 𓆸

THE VILLAGE GREEN

ABBOTS BROMLEY, STAFFORDSHIRE • ABINGER HAMMER, SURREY
BLETCHINGLEY, SURREY • CHIDDINGFOLD, SURREY • CHRISTLETON, CHESHIRE
DUFTON, CUMBRIA • HUSTHWAITE, NORTH YORKSHIRE • LAVENHAM, SUFFOLK
MILBURN, CUMBRIA • MONKS ELEIGH, SUFFOLK • NEW BUCKENHAM, NORFOLK
RIPLEY, NORTH YORKSHIRE • ROMALDKIRK, DURHAM • TURTON, LANCASHIRE
WICKHAMBREAUX, KENT • WIDECOMBE–IN–THE–MOOR DEVON

T O COME ACROSS a green or square is to find the heart of the village. Each green is given its own unique character by the surrounding buildings and landscape, and it will have been the focus of village life for centuries. Synonymous with the reassuring solidity of a weathered market cross or war memorial, greens and squares may, in certain seasons, echo to the music and stamping boots of morris dancing, the excitement of a fair or the crackle of a bonfire.

Most greens and squares began as communal areas that served the village as a whole. Not many written records survive, but it is clear that these common areas are generally very old. There is considerable variation in the character and shape of greens, but rectangular or triangular plans are common. Few have survived unaltered and many have been transformed by the encroachment of roads and houses, or lost altogether.

The erection of buildings or other structures on a green was, in theory, strictly limited to those that served a communal purpose, such as a church, market cross, smithy and sometimes a school. However, if a villager built a cottage on the green and was not challenged, he or she was allowed to remain there thanks to 'squatters' rights'.

Punishment of wrongdoers was frequently carried out on the village green or in the market place, and an Act of 1405 laid down that stocks should be provided in every village. Made by the village carpenter and blacksmith, they proved a cheap and effective means of restraint and punishment. A four-hour stretch in them for drunkenness, vagrancy or blasphemy was not uncommon up until Victorian times. Other miscreants, with their backs bare, might suffer at the whipping post, which often formed part of the stocks. A more lasting memorial to the troublemaker is the village lock-up or jail, which was generally built of stone and often occupied a place on or close to the green.

Most villages had a manorial pound: a gated enclosure constructed from timber, stone or thick hedges that was used to contain livestock that had strayed. It was an essential structure in medieval times, when few animals were kept fenced in. Fines had to be paid by owners to retrieve their animals. There was also sometimes a pond or well and, in later times, a pump to serve the needs of the villagers and to provide water for their sheep, goats and other livestock, which grazed on the green along with geese and ducks.

In the fourteenth century, Edward III introduced a statute to encourage the practice of archery, and many of the archers who went to fight abroad were trained at butts on village greens.

Those villages located where several roads met formed a focal point for trade for the surrounding countryside, and frequently became the site of weekly markets or annual fairs. The right to hold such an event was granted to a medieval town corporation or lord of the manor by royal charter. The charter frequently specified the day on which the market or fair was to be held so that it did not coincide with another local market. Medieval law also commonly limited the proximity of markets to intervals of not less than 6⅔ miles (about 10.5 kilometres). This distance was based on the fact that the average person could walk twenty miles in a day: a third of the day would be spent walking to the market, a third of it was spent there and the final third was spent travelling home. However, those who were tempted by the public house or inn might not make it home until the following day.

The seventeenth-century market house at New Buckenham in Norfolk stands within a well-kept green. It is built on nine wooden columns and the central one once served as the village whipping post. On market days the upper storey provided shade and shelter for the stallholders below.

Between 1198 and 1483, 2,400 grants for markets and fairs were made by the Crown, and over half of these were made before 1275. Manorial lords found it profitable to promote markets because they could exact tolls from stallholders and make money selling their surplus goods. However, the ravages of the Black Death reduced England's population by about a third, and many markets died along with the population.

A medieval market cross still stands in the centre of many villages. In their size and design crosses reflected the status of the market, and acted as a symbol of authority by marking the spot where itinerant traders could sell their wares. Some were like churchyard crosses: the cross or lantern at the head of the shaft was said to emphasise the Christian nature of honest dealing. At particularly successful markets, the cross was sometimes enclosed in an elaborate building that provided shelter for the traders. As the Middle Ages progressed, market houses were sometimes built to house the stalls, booths and pens used in the running of the market.

Medieval markets sold the essentials of everyday life and were held at least weekly. Fairs, which were generally annual events, offered the excitement of goods from much further

afield, such as exotic spices, coloured cloth and fine metalware. Fairs offered a mixture of business and pleasure and, within the generally insular society of the village, a chance to meet new people. There must have been fun and gossip as well as entertainment provided by jugglers, side shows, acrobats, dancing bears and the display of human 'freaks'.

The North Yorkshire village of Ripley was remodelled in the early nineteenth century, but one can still stand by a small enclosed field and enjoy the blend of countryside and fine architecture.

Many fairs originated in the thirteenth and fourteenth centuries and, like markets, were established as an exclusive right by royal charter, which also specified the fair's duration and date. This frequently coincided with the 'feriae' or feast day of the patron saint of the village church, a holy day when labourers had time off. Although the venue for fair and market was sometimes the same, fairs were bigger events and often took place on the outskirts of the village. In some places, a fair house, in which equipment could be kept, was built on the site, and the lessee paid a rent to the charter owner. In return he collected money from the tolls paid by traders.

Fairs were not only held to sell goods and livestock. Statutes were laid down in Elizabeth I's reign which established annual meetings or 'hiring' fairs at which men and women presented themselves for employment, wages were agreed and disputes were settled. Often called 'mop' fairs, they are said to take their name from the fact that domestic servants advertised the job that they wanted by carrying mops or other instruments of their trade.

Many of the festivals and celebrations of recent times stem from earlier, pagan belief and superstition. The celebration of May Day superseded the Celtic ceremony of Beltane, in which the sun was honoured by the burning of great bonfires. Both ceremonies heralded the beginning of summer. The maypole, originally a tree stripped of bark and painted with brightly coloured stripes, is a symbol that stands out clearly in many minds as the epitome of English country life. However, the festivities we see today, which include the crowning of the May Queen, dancing and the use of garlands of spring flowers as decoration, are a Victorian revival of a pagan ceremony.

The day now known as Halloween, which falls on 31 October, is the eve of the Celtic New Year and was the occasion for the spirits of the dead to be welcomed back to earth by the lighting of bonfires. The Anglican Church, always keen to divert attention from such pagan rituals, used the failure of the plot by the Catholic Guy Fawkes to blow up the king and parliament, to create a new celebration in the calendar: bonfire night on 5 November.

Most celebrations had strong links with the farming year but still reflected the important days of the Celtic calendar, such as the summer and winter solstices and the spring and autumn equinoxes. Marking the climax of the farming year was 'harvest home', which came after virtually everyone in the village had participated in the huge task of gathering in the harvest. Labourers were generally badly paid and farmers were frequently resented but, after the harvest, the farmer provided a sumptuous meal, jugs of beer and music for everyone to enjoy. In what was generally a hard life, far removed from romantic notions of the country, feasts like these were times of great merriment and excitement for the entire farming community.

The first Monday after Twelfth Night was Plough Monday, which saw the resumption of labour after the Christmas holiday. Farm labourers dragged a plough dressed in ribbons and other decorations round the village collecting money. Before the Reformation in the sixteenth century, the money was used to buy 'ploughlights', which the men kept burning before certain images in the church to obtain a blessing for their work. Later, it was spent on celebration in the public house.

Another custom, which is still practised in some parts of the country, is 'beating the bounds'. This was adapted from the traditional festival of the Rogation, which has its origins in the eighth century. The clergy, accompanied by the church officers and villagers, walk the boundaries of their parish and, using willow wands, beat the bounds. The ceremony was intended as a supplication for a good harvest but, more practically, the custom was a way of checking that boundary markers had not been moved and that no new buildings had been erected without permission.

In the past many festivals and celebrations were accompanied by morris men, who performed a number of folkdances. The origins of morris dancing are unclear. Some believe it stems from pagan rituals; others connect the term 'morris' with a corruption of 'Moorish', suggesting that the Moors brought the dance to Europe from North Africa. Alternatively it may have its roots in medieval court dances. During Victorian times the tradition almost died, but both the music and the dances were written down and later revived so that today morris dancers are a common sight on many a village green.

Flemish weavers settled in Lavenham in Suffolk in the fourteenth century and, as it became increasingly prosperous as a centre of the wool trade, new buildings were erected by the weavers, merchants and shopkeepers. Luckily, when decline came, Lavenham escaped the subsequent rebuilding suffered in so many other places, and a huge number of medieval buildings survive.

Although now a village, in the Middle Ages Lavenham was a market town. The lanes and streets around the market place have names like Lady Street, Water Street, so called because a river ran alongside it, and Shilling Street, which takes its name from a Flemish weaver called Schylling. In the late eighteenth century an author and engraver, Isaac Taylor, lived there, and it was his daughter Jane who wrote the nursery rhyme 'Twinkle, twinkle, little star.' Even the weavers' cottages have remained intact, and many display in their plasterwork such craft symbols as the fleur-de-lys, spur-rowel and mitre. The old wool hall is now part of the Swan Hotel, the cellars of which are said to date back to the fourteenth century. ❧

In Lavenham's thirteenth-century market place, the colour-washed buildings are vibrant in the sun. The market place is dominated by the fine, late fifteenth-century, timber-framed guildhall of the Guild of Corpus Christi, which was one of the four social and religious guilds in Lavenham when the wool trade was flourishing. It was from the guildhall that wealthy master clothiers controlled the trade. Later, the building served variously as a prison, a workhouse and a wool store. Today, it holds exhibitions on local history, farming and industry. There is also a walled garden with dye plants, and a nineteenth-century lock-up and mortuary. ❧

From the early Middle Ages farming and tin-mining provided a livelihood for those who lived in the area surrounding Widecombe-in-the-Moor in Devon, and the annual fair was vital for the sale of cattle, sheep and ponies. The village was made famous by a song called 'Widecombe Fair', which was written down and published by the vicar of another parish and tells of the adventures of Tom Cobleigh, his friends and a poor grey mare who had to carry them on their journey. In local parts it was said that to be able to sing the chorus was a test of sobriety:

Tom Pearce, Tom Pearce, lend me thy grey mare
(All along, down along, out along lea)
Fer I want to go to Widecombe fair
Wi' Bill Brewer, Jan Stewer, Peter Gurney,
Peter Davy, Dan'l Whiddon, 'Arry 'Awkes,
Ol' Uncle Tom Cobleigh an' all…

Once a market town belonging to the abbey of Burton-upon-Trent, Abbots Bromley in Staffordshire has a butter cross on its village green. These polygonal roofed shelters were provided by local benefactors in late medieval and Tudor times for the trading of butter and other produce.

Abbots Bromley is famous for its Horn Dance. Performed in September, it is said to be unique in Europe and probably dates back to prehistoric times. The six sets of reindeer horns worn by the dancers are of Saxon origin and are kept in the village church of St Nicholas. Carried on their shoulders by 'Deer-Men', the horns are blessed before use. All the characters involved in the dance wear Tudor dress and include a Fool, a Hobby-Horse, Maid Marian – the Man Woman – and a Bowman as well as two musicians. Horns are regarded as an ancient symbol of natural power and the Horn Dance at Abbots Bromley is probably a version of a 'beating the bounds' ceremony. The dancers perform at various points round the village and at nearby estates, with the high point coming when the Deer-Men lower their horns and engage in mock combat.

The village of Bletchingley in Surrey possessed a market before 1262, when the profits from stalls and shops were rated at £2. Its site was on the single main street, which used to broaden out near the church into a typical funnel-shaped market place, but which is now partly encroached upon by tile-hung houses and shops. The Domesday Book records that the manor was held by the de Clare family. Soon after the Conquest a castle was built and by the early thirteenth century it had become a fortified town or borough. In addition to its successful market, permission to hold an annual fair was granted to Gilbert de Clare in 1283. However, the death of the last de Clare in 1314 probably contributed to the subsequent decline of Bletchingly from town back to village.

Surrounded by a low fence, the green at Husthwaite is a tiny triangle, with a sign-post, tree and seat. Unusually in this area of generally stone houses, those at Husthwaite are of brick, and one cottage is half-timbered. Dominating the green is the church of St Nicholas, which has Norman masonry in the nave, chancel and the lower part of the west tower, and a doorway of the first half of the twelfth century. The village name is derived from the Saxon hús or 'house' and thwaite, a Norman word meaning 'clearing'.

Standing close to the edge of the North York Moors National Park, the Hambledon hills stretch northwards from Husthwaite and are the backdrop to the 314-foot (96-metre)-long White Horse, which was incised in the hillside in 1857. Below it stands the ruin of Byland Abbey, which is now in the care of English Heritage. To the west runs a Roman road and, just above the village, Beacon Banks, which take their name from the time in 1588 when they were the site of a beacon set up to warn of the approach of the Spanish Armada.

In the compact village of Monks Eleigh in Suffolk a small green runs towards the church of St Peter between rows of cottages. The parish pump bears the inscription: 'This well was made and pump erected 1854 for the use of the inhabitants of Monks Eleigh out of the proceeds of the sale of some parish property. Joseph Makin Guardian of the Poor'. Its lower half bears the stern warning: 'Take notice that boys or other persons damaging this pump will be prosecuted as the law directs.' Cast-iron village pumps such as this were once a common sight across England. Many were erected after the introduction of the Public Health (Water) Act of 1878, which required that all new rural housing had to be built near to a water supply. These Victorian pumps frequently replaced a well, and bore the name of a benefactor. Some villages also benefited from drinking fountains and water troughs for livestock. ❦

Ripley in North Yorkshire has a vaguely continental air due to the fact that it was rebuilt by the lord of the manor, Sir William Amcotts Ingilby, on the lines of a typical French village. The process began in 1827, and one building of 1854 bears the inscription

'Hôtel de Ville'. However, the cobbled square retained its old market cross, village stocks and a life-size stone boar. This symbolised the granting of Ripley to Thomas Ingilby in the fourteenth century after he had saved Edward III from being attacked by a charging boar in Knaresborough Forest. Beyond the square is a fifteenth-century gateway leading to the castle where, during the Civil War, Oliver Cromwell demanded shelter following the battle of Marston Moor. William Ingilby had gone to fight on the Royalist side and so it was Lady Ingilby who kept guard over the castle, threatening to shoot the Roundhead leader and his men if they did not behave.

Lying low in the Kent landscape, the small village of Wickhambreaux stands on the banks of a tributary of the River Stour. At its centre it has a triangular green shaded by lime and chestnut trees. Around it are cottages, the rectory and a fifteenth-century house built mainly of flint and brick. An avenue of trees leads from the northwest corner of the green to the church of St Andrew. Nearby, to the west, is the town of Canterbury which became the centre of the English Church after St Augustine's mission in 597. In 1170 Archbishop Thomas à Becket was murdered in the cathedral after he had quarrelled with his patron Henry II and, in the Middle Ages, his shrine attracted vast numbers of pilgrims. ⅋

In the shadow of Great Dun Fell lies the Cumbrian village of Milburn, its slate roofs merging with the thunderous clouds that sweep the hills. This is a village that seems to have been built to a plan rather than in a higgledy-piggledy fashion. Facing inwards, rugged red- and pink-tinged sandstone houses closely border the rectangular village green on all four sides, with few gaps in between, so access has to be gained via narrow entrances at the four corners. It has been suggested that this design made it easier to defend the village against marauders. However, a more likely explanation – especially as the church is outside this village centre – is that it was intended to contain livestock. The green itself is split up by paths and roadways and extends to some 4½ acres (1.8 hectares), with a school at one end that dates from 1851. Although the area is peaceful now, it has not always been so; nearby Howgill Castle originally consisted of two fourteenth-century fortified homesteads built to protect the inhabitants from Scottish raids.

The stocks (left) at Turton in Lancashire have been carefully preserved in a small garden in the village. Until Victorian times a spell in the stocks was a common punishment for offenders, whose ankles were held in slots between a pair of boards that were clamped together. These were secured by a hinge at one end and a large iron clasp and padlock at the other. Behind the stocks there was a low bench and, in some villages, a whipping post. Details of the sentence were often hung on an adjacent noticeboard, and the offenders would be left to sit in the stocks for a humiliating period, during which time they were exposed to the ridicule and sometimes the missiles – which could include rotten fruit – of the local community. In some places the stocks were designed to accommodate several miscreants at a time. ❧

Abinger Hammer in Surrey is one of a pair of villages; Abinger Common lies a short distance away in the hills to the south. The River Tillingbourne runs through the length of Abinger Hammer's green (left) beside a road bordered by tile-hung and weather-boarded houses, shops and a blacksmith's forge. The green is now preserved as a memorial to the men who died in the First World War. During the summer, cricket is played on the green – as it is in many villages across the country.

Amongst those who have gained inspiration from the area was the author E. M. Forster, who paid frequent visits to his aunt at Abinger until her death in 1924 when he made it his own home for more than twenty years. Nearby, on the lower slopes of the North Downs at Abinger Roughs, is a large granite cross marking the spot where Samuel Wilberforce, son of the slave-trade abolitionist William Wilberforce, was thrown from his horse and killed in 1873. ❧

The shingled well house (above) at Christleton in Cheshire was probably designed by John Douglas, who was involved with many commissions at the nearby Eaton Hall estate, which belonged to the Duke of Westminster's family. Christleton has one of Cheshire's few greens, which extends to an area of some 2½ acres (1 hectare), and has at its edge half-timbered Victorian almshouses beside a pond. ❧

The maroon-painted Georgian stone pump with its ball finial is the most striking feature on the green in the Cumbrian village of Dufton. Cottages of the middle and late-eighteenth century surround the broad, oblong green, which has an avenue of trees down the middle. The green is very similar in size to the one at Milburn, some 4 miles (6.5 kilometres) away to the north but, although surrounded by cottages and farm buildings, it is less enclosed. Dufton lies at the foot of Dufton Pike which, at the western edge of the Pennines, rises 1,578 feet (481 metres) and is one of the few real peaks in the Pennine chain. The Pennine Way loops past the eastern edge of the village and, if followed northwards, leads eventually to Hadrian's Wall. The wall was built between A.D.122 and 123 and stretches 73 miles (117 kilometres) across England to divide the 'civilised' word of the Romans from the northern tribes beyond. Now a World Heritage Site, the wall is in the care of English Heritage.

In a small valley, sheltered from the surrounding fells and moors, Romaldkirk stands at the heart of Teesdale on the eastern side of the Pennines in Durham. The village takes its name from St Romald, the infant son of a ninth century Northumbrian king, who lived for only three days. It is a place of grey stone houses and cottages haphazardly scattered around a number of well-tended greens that are set off by gardens, trees and stone walls. The Georgian rectory and church of St Romald preside over the lowest green. The church has Saxon origins, although the present nave and north aisle date from the twelfth century and the tower is fifteenth century. Beside the churchyard a path leads down towards the River Tees and Romaldkirk Mill, which fell out of use around a hundred years ago. There was once a brewery that supplied the village pubs, including the eighteenth-century Rose and Crown, which was once a flourishing coaching inn. In front of the pub stand the remains of the old village stocks.

November 5th, the anniversary of the failed attempt by Guy Fawkes to blow up Parliament in 1605, is celebrated each year on the village green in Chiddingfold, Surrey, with a torchlight procession, a bonfire and fireworks. In 1929 the village policeman, who was suspected of having set the bonfire alight prematurely, was pitched into the pond. The angry scenes that followed led to two hundred and fifty police officers being sent to the village, and it was reputedly the occasion of the last reading of the Riot Act in the United Kingdom.

In the fourteenth century Chiddingfold received a Royal Charter granting the privilege of an annual fair, on or about the Feast of the Nativity of the Blessed Virgin Mary, as well as a weekly market every Thursday. Until 1812 the market house stood, with the village stocks close by, on the site of what is today the blacksmith's forge on the village green. It was on the green on 21 July 1552 that Edward VI stopped with a retinue of some four thousand, including high officers of state, courtiers, peers and men-at-arms, so it must be assumed that the green was somewhat larger than it is today. ❧

THE VILLAGE CHURCH

———— ❦ ————

ALFRISTON, EAST SUSSEX • BISLEY, GLOUCESTERSHIRE • BRENT TOR, DEVON
HAMBLEDEN, BUCKINGHAMSHIRE • HAWORTH, WEST YORKSHIRE
IVYCHURCH, KENT • KELMSCOTT, OXFORDSHIRE • LAXTON, NOTTINGHAMSHIRE
MUCH HADHAM, HERTFORDSHIRE • NETHER WINCHENDON, BUCKINGHAMSHIRE
SHERE, SURREY • STOKE, DEVON • TONG, SHROPSHIRE
WEOBLEY, HEREFORD AND WORCESTER • WEST TANFIELD, NORTH YORKSHIRE
WIDECOMBE-IN-THE-MOOR, DEVON • WOOLPIT, SUFFOLK

T HE CHURCH HOLDS a position unlike that of any other building or institution in the village, and has been at the centre of the community for centuries. A place of refuge, joy and sorrow, its only rival in reflecting the full gamut of human emotion is the village pub. The church is likely to be the oldest building in the village and at one time the only stone structure other than the manor house. Today, for anyone who ventures inside, there is the same feeling of sanctity that has existed for centuries. By lifting the latch on the heavy timber door, the visitor steps from one world to another, to be engulfed by a hushed calm and the scent of polish, flowers and slight mustiness.

A great deal of the history of a village can be gleaned from its church, as the lives, loves and deaths of its men, women and children are recorded on the memorials and gravestones, and in parish registers that have been kept since 1538. However, the history of most village churches is likely to stretch back farther than any records. It seems that the first Christian communities may have been established in England before the end of the second century, but the age of church-building in which our present churches have their roots came later, when the Christian faith was established in the late sixth and early seventh centuries by missionaries who often built their new churches on sites that had been considered sacred before the arrival of Christianity. By 660, only the people of Sussex and the Isle of Wight were still pagan.

The parish system developed in the ninth and tenth centuries and is the smallest unit of ecclesiastical administration. As the church was often the largest building in a parish it served a dual role, with the nave becoming a meeting place for secular activities as well as religious ones. Plays, dances and feasts were all held there. The chancel, the upkeep of which was administered by the priest, was regarded as the most sacred area, and a screen was often erected to divide it from the nave, which was the responsibility of the parishioners. In many cases, part of the church or a side chapel belonged to the manorial family and contained its dead, its memorials and private pews which, in the eighteenth and nineteenth centuries, were frequently made more comfortable with the provision of a stove or fireplace.

In times of crisis the church was a place of refuge as well as prayer and, in areas subject to flooding, it is common to find the church on high ground. It was also sanctuary to fugitives and criminals who, once they entered the churchyard, could stay in safety for a statutory forty days. Originating in pagan times, this right was confirmed when Ethelbert, King of Kent, issued laws on the sanctity of churches shortly after his conversion to Christianity in 597. Violation of this sanctity could lead to severe punishment or even excommunication. If, after forty days, the fugitive refused to submit to trial, he was compelled to take an oath before the coroner that he would flee the country by a particular port, proceeding there on foot, clad in a garment of sackcloth. Sanctuary for criminal offences was abolished in 1623, and for civil purposes in 1773.

While the population could enjoy the benefits of the church in terms of security and religious faith, these came at a price. A tenth of every parishioner's income in cash, crops or animals had to be paid to the church in 'tithes' to support it and the clergy, a practice begun in the ninth century and still part of the law (in the form of a cash payment) as late as 1936.

The Golden Chapel of St Bartholomew's church at Tong in Shropshire is roofed by fan-vaulting that was once gilded. It was built in 1515 as a chantry chapel in which mass would be said for the repose of the souls of the church's founders.

The fact that church and manor house frequently stand close to one another is no accident. From Saxon times, the village church was frequently built on the lord's land and the parish priest often enjoyed the protection and patronage of the landowner. In return, the lord would collect the income from the tithes and would employ the priest as his chaplain. However, many priests lived in houses that were small and squalid. These were often surrounded by a farmyard, as an area of 'glebe' land was set aside for them to produce their own food.

Others directly involved in the work of the parish included the parish clerk, who prepared for services, rang the service bell and led the responses, and the sexton, who dug the graves and cleaned the church. The administration of the church, however, concerned far more than just the building itself. Churchwardens were appointed by the parish and severe fines were imposed on anyone refusing to serve as warden. By the time of Elizabeth I, they were responsible for everything from the appointment of parish officers to the destruction of vermin, as well as the repair of local roads and bridges. Churchwardens also had to report to the bishop on the general behaviour of the priest.

The sound of church bells ringing across the countryside is highly evocative. Bells are consecrated and inscribed with ritual words and a cross and, in the superstitious times of medieval England, their clamour was intended to clear the atmosphere of malevolent forces and open a channel to God. During violent storms, which were held to be the work of demonic forces, the bells were sounded to quell mischief. As recently as the Second World War their sound was a warning of invasion.

As well as being rung before each service, bells are used to celebrate marriage and victory. The 'passing bell' was once tolled when someone was dying, since it was believed that the soul was released from the body at the moment of death and that demons might seize it. Although a variation of this custom survives in many churches, now the bell is tolled after death.

The rituals of burial and the trappings that accompany it are highly visible elements in any church. The wealthy have frequently found a resting place inside the building, with elaborate memorials that record their lives. Just as fascinating is the churchyard where, frequently under the shade of ancient yew trees, headstones and tombs are revealing in their inscriptions and enhance the picturesque setting of the church.

Water and salt, the latter a symbol of preservation, were used in the consecration of churchyards. Often, the shaded area on the north side of the church was left unconsecrated because it was popularly associated with forces of evil. Here, the surface may be uneven and cluttered with unmarked graves since it was generally the last resting place of unbaptised babies, paupers, thieves and those who had died in mortal sin, such as suicides. As a consequence of this, the ground on the favoured south side gradually became higher as each generation laid their dead above those of former ages.

Early Saxon churches were simple wooden structures built as a shelter for the priest and the altar. This shelter became the chancel and, as the number of worshippers grew, they too needed protection from the elements, so a large adjoining building, or nave, was constructed, often of a different size and style from that of the chancel. These early wooden churches soon gave way to more substantial stone structures, often reflecting the best materials found in the surrounding landscape.

Few of the churches that we see today reflect just one period or material, and often such things as bricks, stones and tiles from earlier buildings, including Roman ones, have been incorporated. A great number of parish churches were enlarged and modernised during the twelfth century. The prosperous thirteenth century represented the apogee of English medieval architecture. Money for such work frequently came from those wishing to insure their souls, but, just as today, constant efforts had to be made to replenish church coffers through fund-raising activities such as gatherings and festivals, the performance of parish plays, and the holding of 'church ales' – the equivalent of the modern church bazaar.

The basic design of chancel and nave was expanded with the addition of aisles and a

tower which, as well as containing bells, sometimes served as beacon, observation post and even a strong-room for valuables. As the tallest structure in most villages, the church tower was regarded as a prestigious symbol. This resulted in a certain amount of competition between villages, and attempts to build ever taller towers led to a number of collapses.

The armoured figure in alabaster of Sir Richard Vernon, who was a Speaker of the House of Commons in the sixteenth century, lies next to that of his wife, Margaret, in St Bartholomew's church in Tong. Medieval effigies such as these can be found in churches across the country.

The same local pride often led to the interior of the church being richly embellished. In Tudor times, some country churches still had unflagged earthen floors strewn with straw or rushes. However, those in areas where the wool trade flourished, such as East Anglia and the Cotswolds, were richly decorated with colourful floor tiles. Wall-paintings, carvings and stained-glass windows were used to illustrate Bible stories and, at the same time, uplift the congregation. Sadly, though, much of this decorative art was swept away after Henry VIII confiscated church wealth during the Reformation of the mid-sixteenth century. More damage was done by the Puritans in the middle of the seventeenth century, when many inscriptions and wall paintings were painted over, stained-glass windows were smashed and statues were destroyed. Much ancient church structure and decoration was also lost in Victorian times, thanks to over-enthusiastic remodelling and repair. Amazingly, though, much of value has survived and many village churches reflect a wonderful combination of periods and styles.

At the bottom of a valley in the Chiltern hills in Buckinghamshire, lies Hambleden. St Mary's church stands in the centre of the village beside a small triangular green, surrounded by flint and brick cottages. In Norman times the church had a central tower, but this collapsed in 1703. The present tower was built in 1721 and heightened in 1883. The church contains panels from around 1525 bearing the arms of Cardinal Wolsey. After his failure to procure papal consent for Henry VIII's divorce from Catherine of Aragon, Wolsey was dismissed from his position as Chancellor and had to yield up much of his vast wealth to the king. He was subsequently arrested for high treason and died on his way to trial.

A gabled lych gate leads into the churchyard which contains the grave of Viscount Hambleden who, as well as being the lord of the manor and a politician, is better known today as the newsagent and bookseller W. H. Smith.

Above the church is the tall, gabled seventeenth-century manor house in which James Thomas Brudenell was born. As Lord Cardigan, Brudenell led the disastrous 'Charge of the Light Brigade' at Balaclava in 1854 during the Crimean War. The ill-fated charge was immortalised in the poem by Tennyson.

The painting of ceilings in bright colours, such as these at St Mary's church at Hambleden, was common before the Reformation. In the Middle Ages colour and gilding were employed extensively in church interiors, not just on ceilings but on plaster walls and stonework pillars. Paintings that depicted biblical scenes helped to convey the Christian story to a congregation that was largely illiterate. ❧

Although clocks existed in the fourteenth century, it was the seventeenth century before the clocks on village churches had dials. Previously, figures called clock jacks struck the hour and its quarters on a bell or bells. Monasteries used sundials to show the eight hours of service or liturgy, the pattern of which was determined daily by the hours of daylight. Some churches had several dials, each of which was used during a different time of the year.

The church of St Peter and St Paul at Weobley in Herefordshire has both a clock and a sundial. The church spire rises from a tower supported by flying buttresses, and dates from the fourteenth century. ❧

ONE DAY TELLETH ANOTHER, AND·
ONE NIGHT CERTIFIETH ANOTHER

The village of Much Hadham in Hertfordshire was home to the sculptor Henry Moore for over forty years, and his work is in evidence at the church of St Andrew. Beside the west door below the tower are Moore's heads of a king and a queen (right), which replaced two earlier cement casts in 1953. Standing away from the main street of sixteenth- and seventeenth-century cottages and Georgian houses, the church is of flint and has a tall spike of a spire. St Andrew's may date from the twelfth century, but the chancel was rebuilt around 1220 and further work was carried out over a considerable period. The present clerestory, roofs and south porch were not built until the fifteenth century.

The manor was once owned by the Bishops of London and the long brick palace to the north of the churchyard was the incumbent Bishop's country residence. Much Hadham was also the birthplace of Edmund Tudor, the father of Henry VII, the first of England's Tudor monarchs. ❧

Figures of human, animal and grotesque form are present in an enormous number of churches and were frequently carved as part of the exterior stonework, as at the church of St Michael at Laxton in Nottinghamshire. Often these gargoyles are spouts that project from the parapet of a wall or tower and throw rainwater clear of the building. There is no doubt that many medieval masons and churchmen had a sense of humour, for such work occasionally shows figures in not altogether decent attitudes.

Heads, angels and animals are also depicted in mouldings over windows and doors and, although such carvings may not seem to fulfil a practical role, there was often a reason for their presence. Superstition was strong in the Middle Ages, and such devices were seen as protection against evil spirits and witchcraft. As a result, they are found on houses and farm buildings as well as churches. Finials on spires had a similar function, and the weathercock, a common feature above many churches, may have been positioned there to do more than indicate the direction of the wind. As a symbol of vigilance, the cock may have been intended to guard against the approach of hostile spirits. 🎄

The Anglo-Saxon name for Woolpit in Suffolk was Wolfpeta, which meant a pit for trapping wolves, and it is claimed that the last wolf in Suffolk was killed in the village. Woolpit contains a mixture of timber-framed Tudor and brick Georgian houses, but the eleventh-century church of St Mary is built of stone and flint. The church boasts a steeple that is 140 feet (42 metres) high. The tower and spire were rebuilt in 1853, having collapsed after a storm.

The fifteenth-century south porch has two-storeys, which is typical of the area's churches in this period, and has elaborately carved stone. Inside, the double hammerbeam roof is decorated with angels, their wings outstretched, and is one of the best in East Anglia. Within the nave the pews are carved with poppy heads, saints and animals, while the pulpit was designed by George Gilbert Scott, the son of the Victorian architect of the same name. The rood canopy was erected below the east window around 1875 and was probably brought from another church.

In the 1640s, William Dowsing, a religious fanatic acting on behalf of Parliament during the Civil War, destroyed much of value in St Mary's, including eighty of the church's pictures and statues.

The tiny church of St Michael de Rupe at Brent Tor was once a landmark for mariners returning to the southern port of Plymouth Sound. The building is perched 1,100 feet (330 metres) above sea level on a cliff of ancient volcanic rock at the western edge of Dartmoor. Folklore suggests that it was built by a merchant who, having survived a terrible storm at sea, vowed to build a church on the first land he saw. Others believe it to have been constructed as an act of contrition by Robert Giffard, a Norman landowner.

Said to be the fourth-smallest church in the country, it measures just 40 feet by 14 feet (12 metres by 4 metres) and its tower is 32 feet (10 metres) high. Records for the church date it from before 1150, and it once belonged to Tavistock Abbey, which established an annual fair at Brentor in 1232. The present building, however, dates mainly from the thirteenth century. 🐾

A hexagonal 'poor souls' light' (left) stands in the churchyard of All Saints church at Bisley in Gloucestershire. When masses were said for the poor, candles were placed in the light. Dating from the late thirteenth century, it is believed to be the only outdoor example in England, and is said to be built over a well down which a clergyman had fallen.

At the centre of a large parish, the church dates from the thirteenth and fourteenth centuries, but by the early nineteenth century it had fallen into such a state of disrepair that the nave roof was held up by a tree. It was restored in 1863 by Thomas Keble, brother to the more famous John Keble (see page 131), and his curate, the Reverend Lowder. Thomas Keble was followed as vicar by his son, and the family occupied the vicarage until 1902. The Victorian period was one of unparalleled church-building and restoration, and the Kebles did much to revive the fortunes of the Church in their immediate area.

A gabled thirteenth-century bellcote stands above St George's church, which lies at one end of the Oxfordshire village of Kelmscott. Bellcotes often contain just one bell and are generally found at smaller churches and nonconformist chapels.

In a corner of the churchyard is a stone monument designed by Philip Webb for his close friend and colleague, the artist William Morris, who died on 3 October 1896 at the age of sixty-two. Morris's funeral was a simple ceremony, with his body carried on an open haycart festooned with vines, alder and bulrushes. In the village is a group of cottages built in 1902 by Morris's widow, Jane, as a memorial to him. ❧

The church of St Bartholomew at Tong in Shropshire has been called the 'village Westminster Abbey' because of its wealth of fine monuments. It was built after Elizabeth de Pembruge founded a chantry college in memory of her husband Sir Fulke in 1410. The church is of red sandstone and is notable for its impressive effigies and monuments, which were often prepared a considerable time before the subject's death. Three-dimensional effigies (left), carved in alabaster, stone, wood and – for the most noble – bronze, were normally placed on a tomb chest. In medieval times decorated floor tiles were used sparingly in most churches, and are generally found in important areas such as around the altar and in chancels and chapels. The fleur-de-lys was a popular design (above) amongst other, often geometric, patterns usually of red and yellow. The carved wooden choir stalls (right) are decorated with angels.

Lying in the Dartmoor National Park in Devon, Widecombe-in-the-Moor's church is built of granite in the perpendicular style. The interior is long and low, which is typical of West Country churches. The nave and aisles are of equal height and have plastered wagon roofs, while the six bays have octagonal granite piers. In the tall west tower, four painted boards dated 1786 display verses describing the events that took place during a service on Sunday, 21 October, 1638. As a thunderstorm raged outside, one of the pinnacles of the tower was struck by lightning and fell through the roof. Four members of the congregation were killed and many others were injured. A survivor described seeing a mysterious figure with a cloven hoof, and from this grew the legend that the accident was caused by the Devil, who had tethered his horse to the pinnacle while he went inside to claim the souls of a group of men who were playing cards.

At Stoke, on Devon's Atlantic coast near the jagged cliffs of Hartland Quay, stands a fourteenth-century church dedicated to St Nectan. At some 130 feet (39 metres) high, its tower is the tallest in Devon and is said to have been built as a landmark for sailors. The original church, built in 1055, was replaced by the present building in 1360 and embellished in the late fifteenth century. Further reconstruction was carried out in 1848. St Nectan's contains fine and unusually high wagon roofs that are typical of North Devon's churches. Extending the entire width of the church is a late fifteenth-century rood screen, and above the north porch is a chamber in which the priest once slept. Northeast of the church stands a house built in 1779 on the site of what was once Hartland Abbey. The abbey was founded before the Norman Conquest as a college for secular cannons and, during the reign of Henry II in the twelfth century, was refounded as an Augustinian abbey; it was later dissolved by Henry VIII in 1535. ❧

It is the parsonage (above), rather than the church, that has made Haworth famous as it was here that the Brontë sisters, Charlotte, Emily and Anne, and their brother Branwell, lived from 1820. The present church of St Michael's was not built until 1880.

The three Brontë sisters all left Haworth at various points in their lives, first as pupils and later as teachers and governesses. However, in 1846, they were all back in the village, and the following year Charlotte's *Jane Eyre*, Emily's *Wuthering Heights* and Anne's *Agnes Grey* were published.

The village of Haworth was associated with the weaving industry, and expansion had left it overcrowded. Sanitation was poor and the average age of death was twenty-eight and a half years. By 1849, Branwell, Emily and Anne had all died. Charlotte went on to marry her father's curate, but enjoyed less than a year of married life before her death in 1855. ❧

Alfriston's church of St Andrew stands in the East Sussex valley of the River Cuckmere within an almost circular churchyard. It lies away from the main village beside the river and a broad green called the Tye. Dating from around 1360, the church is built of local knapped flint in the form of a Greek cross - that is a cross with four equal arms - and has a central shingle spire. Architecturally it is an example of the transition from the Decorated to the Perpendicular style. Like many of the churches of Sussex, it has been refurnished, but inside there are high impressive arches and unusual triple sedilia: stone seats used by the celebrant and his two assistants. The church marriage register is said to be the oldest in England and dates from 1504.

There are a number of Saxon burial places close to Alfriston, and over a hundred graves have been excavated, yielding finds such as drinking horns and spearheads. ❧

At one time the congregation was expected to stand throughout a church service and, although low stone benches sometimes ran along the walls of the nave, they were reserved for the aged and infirm. Pews were gradually introduced in the fourteenth century, when the sermon became a more important part of the service. By the fifteenth century pews were commonplace, and were frequently enriched by carvings such as this bench end of a monk playing a harp in the church of St Nicholas at West Tanfield in North Yorkshire. Around the same time, the chancels of many churches were extended and carved wooden stalls for the clergy and choir were introduced. To help the clergy rest during the lengthy services their seats tipped up and had small, frequently highly decorated ledges underneath called 'misericords'. These allowed the priest to prop himself up while appearing to stand. ❧

Lying in the flat open expanse of Romney Marsh in Kent, the village of Ivychurch has a church of around 1360 that is built from a coarse local stone called ragstone. The threat of invasion has always hung over the Marsh, and the tower of St George's church has a beacon turret that served as a lookout post. At one time, most of the Marsh villages were involved with smuggling, and a vault below the church was used by smugglers who emptied coffins of bodies and used them to store their contraband. Once, the sexton turned the rector away, saying: 'Bain't be no service, parson. Pulpit be full o'baccy, and vestry be full o'brandy'.

St George's was restored in the nineteenth century, and again after being damaged during the Second World War. During the war, the upper room of the two-storey battlemented south porch is said to have been used as a food store, and it has also served as the village school. Architecturally the church is in the late Decorated-Perpendicular style, and its large interior has an unspoilt nave and seven arches.

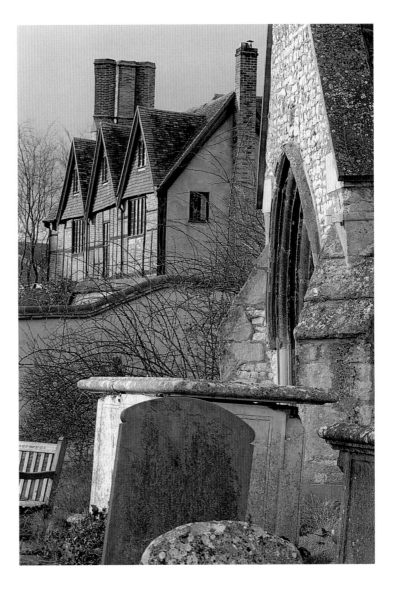

Set at the foot of a steep hill in the valley of the River Thame, the village of Nether (or Lower) Winchendon, is gathered around a small green. Here, alongside sixteenth- and seventeenth-century timber-framed houses, stands the church of St Nicholas. The chancel was rebuilt in 1891, but most of the church remains unspoilt, with a gallery that probably dates from the early nineteenth century, high pews and a large Jacobean pulpit. The base of the tower and part of the north wall are said to date from the eleventh century.

Just beyond the churchyard is the large, gabled manor farmhouse, which has a door dated 1620. A lane from the church leads to the medieval Nether Winchendon House, which was 'gothicised' around 1780. It was once home to Sir Francis Bernard, Governor of New Jersey from 1758 to 1760 and Governor of Massachusetts from 1760 to 1770.

Lying in the valley of the River Tillingbourne, St James's church at Shere dates from around 1190. The gabled lych gate, with a kissing gate beside it (above), was designed by Sir Edwin Lutyens and erected in 1902. Inside on the north wall of the chancel there is a squint window and a quatrefoil, all that remains of an enclosed cell built in 1329 for Christine Carpenter, an anchoress. In the Middle Ages both priests and lay people became anchorites or anchoresses, literally anchoring themselves to the church, giving up the distractions of the world to lead a pious life in the service of God. Christine Carpenter watched the solemn ritual of mass through the narrow slot cut in the church wall and received the sacrament through the quatrefoil. Her only release should have been death, but she managed to endure just three years of enclosure, although she faced excommunication for leaving her self-imposed confinement. ❧

WATERSIDE VILLAGES

ABINGER COMMON, SURREY • ALFRISTON, EAST SUSSEX • ALLERFORD, SOMERSET
BAINBRIDGE, NORTH YORKSHIRE • BIBURY, GLOUCESTERSHIRE • BISLEY, GLOUCESTERSHIRE
CALDBECK, CUMBRIA • CASTLE COMBE, WILTSHIRE • CHEWTON MENDIP, SOMERSET
CHRISTLETON, CHESHIRE • EASTLEACH, GLOUCESTERSHIRE • FRAMPTON ON SEVERN, GLOUCESTERSHIRE
HUTTON-LE-HOLE, NORTH YORKSHIRE • LOWER SLAUGHTER, GLOUCESTERSHIRE • MORLAND, CUMBRIA
POSTBRIDGE, DEVON • UPPER SLAUGHTER, GLOUCESTERSHIRE • WEST TANFIELD, NORTH YORKSHIRE
WHALLEY, LANCASHIRE • WICKHAMBREAUX, KENT

A S THEIR WATER SPLASHES OVER STONES, ripples reflected along the sides of cottage walls, rivers and streams add a sense of history to the hamlets and villages through which they pass. Elsewhere the calm of a pond or the bustle of a canal act as a focus to the eye and draw the inquisitive. The presence of water had a direct effect on where villages formed. Springs represented a reliable source of fresh water, so settlements grew around them and, in time, many of these developed into hamlets, villages or towns.

Centuries later, when streams and rivers began to form an important network of trade and communication routes, communities sprang up close to them. Frequently, these same watercourses delineated territories, and many still mark out parish and county boundaries.

Once, the maintenance of roads was the responsibility of the local manor or parish, with the result that overland routes were far from reliable. For centuries, river travel remained the best way to carry goods over any distance, and many villages benefited from the resultant trade. Across the country, boatmen transported all kinds of goods through areas that lacked decent roads. Small boats could journey far upstream, although navigation was heavily reliant on the tides and the seasons, and boats would frequently have to wait several hours for suitable conditions. Boatmen made use of the force of the incoming tide to travel further upriver than would otherwise have been possible. High tide caused the fresh river water to 'back up', causing a dam effect that pooled deep water upstream.

The boats used have always reflected the needs of the particular waters on which they served. For example, the single-masted wherry was designed to negotiate the shallow lakes and rivers of the Norfolk Broads. When the wind dropped, the crew could use long poles to push the boat along the narrow channels that make up the Broads.

Looking at a river as it trickles through a village today, it can be hard to believe that it was once a thriving trade route. The use of water mills and weirs and developments such as irrigation and land reclamation led to the lowering of water levels as river channels were obstructed. However, it is in recent times that most change has occurred. So much water has been used in the late twentieth century to supply the needs of homes, industry and agriculture that many once-powerful waterways have silted up.

Whether by ford, stepping stones or bridge, people have found a way to cross the waterways that criss-cross the landscape. Fords once represented the only firm crossing points throughout the year and many villages developed around them. Fords were generally to be found at bends in the upper reaches of a river, where the water was at its shallowest. Even when bridges were built nearby, large wagons and carts would often continue to use the ford, particularly where the riverbed had been reinforced with stone.

The earliest surviving bridges are clapper bridges, which were first used in prehistoric times and consist of huge slabs of stone placed over low piers built of boulders or piles of flat stones.

Just as the maintenance and building of medieval roads were the responsibility of each village, the provision of a bridge frequently relied on the goodwill of a wealthy landowner, religious house or merchant, who would see direct benefit from its construction. Sometimes tolls were levied to offset the cost of maintenance and swell the coffers of the patron. The appalling state of English roads only began to improve with the introduction of toll roads under the first Turnpike Act of 1663. A better transport network necessitated more bridges and the late seventeenth century saw bridge-building increase.

Winding through the limestone of the Cumbrian village of Morland, the swiftly running stream or beck is spanned by a simple wooden footbridge.

While the rivers, and later the canals, brought trade and goods to the villages there were other, local activities associated with water. Where no bridge existed ferries were common, and the rights to provide this service were a highly valued source of revenue. Rivers and streams provided both fish and eels, which were taken on lines, in traps or in nets, and sometimes simply by using a barbed trident-like spear to stab them in the mud of ditches. Poachers trespassing on the squire's land risked severe punishment if caught, but their patience was frequently rewarded despite the best efforts of the local bailiffs, who would check the rivers for illegal fish traps. Made of stakes and nets or basketwork, fish traps were often fixed across the channel, and impeded the progress of boatmen, causing them considerable annoyance

Another obstruction to river transport was the weir. Weirs were constructed to hold

back water and so create a reservoir that could drive a mill wheel. The Domesday Survey of 1086 records some 5,624 water mills in England and scores of later mills occupied the sites of their medieval predecessors.

As well as weirs, millers frequently controlled 'flash' locks, which were introduced for the benefit of the boatmen where shallows would otherwise make it difficult to navigate. These locks had the effect of raising the water level in the river to provide a sufficiently large draught for the passage of boats. In some places, flash locks were still in use until the end of the eighteenth century. Much less sophisticated than later canal locks, the central section consisted of a movable barrier. When the barrier was removed, a great volume of water was released and caused a 'flash' which shot the boat downstream. Such an operation required great skill from the boatmen as well as immense patience, because they were frequently at the mercy of the miller who, especially in dry weather, when water was short, would be reluctant to open the lock.

For a boat to travel upstream through the lock it was sometimes hauled by a winch or sheer muscle power supplied by large gangs of men who waited at such points to assist boatmen. Once through, the central barrier was replaced so that the water level rose, allowing the boat to continue over the shallows.

In Elizabeth I's reign the pound lock was introduced. This consisted of a chamber enclosed by two sets of gates fitted with sluices. Compared with flash locks, pound locks

Lying in a shallow valley, the wide greens at the centre of the village of Hutton-le-Hole are divided by Hutton Beck as it makes its journey southwards from the expanse of the North Yorkshire Moors.

had the advantage of saving water, and several rivers were made navigable by their use during the sixteenth and seventeenth centuries.

The introduction of locks and weirs could lead to flooding, which landowners saw as a threat to their land. However, by the seventeenth century landowners had discovered that deliberate and controlled flooding to create water meadows had many benefits. In the southern chalklands, river water not only provided rich nutrients to feed the pastures but had the effect of raising the ground temperature. Soon the practice of flooding was taken up in other areas of the country and extensive networks of ditches and dykes were used to channel water across the meadows. In winter they were flooded to provide spring grazing for sheep, a practice which became especially important during the sheep-farming boom of the seventeenth and early eighteenth centuries. In April the same meadows were flooded to nourish the June hay crop and again afterwards to hasten new growth.

Roman Britain had seen the first development of waterways and the building of canals such as the Car Dyke in south Lincolnshire. The river system was fully extended during a process that began in 1757 with the construction of the first modern English canal: the Sankey Canal in Lancashire. To transform a river into a canal, the river banks had to be reinforced and built up, bends were straightened, riverbeds dredged and weeds cut. These major schemes, which were intended to shorten journey times, provided employment for village people and helped local trade.

Unlike rivers, where boats relied on man or wind power, canals had towpaths along which horses could haul the load. This harnessing of horsepower provided a reliable and cost-effective means of moving goods, which could, for example, travel from Liverpool to London, a distance of 202 miles (325 kilometres) in two days. A single horse towing a barge on a canal was capable of pulling a 50-ton load while a horse drawing a stage wagon on a good macadam road could draw only 2 tons.

These advantages inspired prominent manufacturers and mine owners to back the building of canals, and such schemes gained increasing momentum as the Industrial Revolution of the eighteenth and nineteenth centuries brought huge demand for the movement of goods.

For village men it meant employment as canal cutters or 'navigators', leading to the birth of a new word in the English language: 'navvy'. Other local people found work as lock keepers. Less positive was the effect on local water supplies. Although large catchment reservoirs were built to supply the needs of the canals, many streams were intercepted and rivers tapped, thus draining water from other areas.

With the development of the railways came a much more economic and efficient means of moving goods, and the canal age all but ended in the 1840s, leaving many waterways to fall into stagnant disrepair. In the last twenty years there has been a concerted effort to clear many derelict canals so that boatmen and walkers can again enjoy their calm beauty. England's rivers and streams have also been revived from overuse and abuse, and in many places fish can once again be seen slipping through villages and disappearing between verdant banks bright with flowers and draped in trailing willow fronds.

With a name meaning 'holy' or 'strong', the River Ure begins its journey amongst the Dales of North Yorkshire and, in its middle reaches, flows past the well-wooded hills and fertile water meadows that marked the boundary between the North and West Ridings of Yorkshire. At West Tanfield the broad sweep of the river passes rows of cottages with slate and rich terracotta pantile roofs. Above them stands the tower of St Nicholas church and next to it the Marmion Tower, all that remains of what was once the castle gatehouse. While the tower is thought to date from the fifteenth century, the oldest feature of the church is the south doorway of around 1200. The tombs are impressive and a wrought-iron hearse, with metal spikes or 'prickets' for candles, encloses alabaster effigies of a knight, probably Sir John Marmion, who died in 1387, and his wife. ❧

Castle Combe in Wiltshire (left) lies some 17 miles (27 kilometres) from the coast, but this did not stop it from being transformed into a seaport for the original film version of *Dr Dolittle* starring Rex Harrison. Flowing down to meet the River Avon, the Bybrook runs beside seventeenth-century cottages. The bridge is built with arches of Roman type, and may even have Roman origins. As its name implies, the village nestles in a wooded hollow in a valley or combe and, in a park above the village, there was once a castle. The village was an important centre for the cloth trade and a fifteenth-century market cross is a symbol of its past importance. The money from the wool trade also contributed to the building of the fine medieval church of St Andrew, which features a wonderful range of Gothic architecture. For more than five hundred years the Scrope family owned Castle Combe and one Lady Millicent married Sir John Fastolf who, through Shakespeare's pen, became Falstaff.

Known as Keble's Bridge (above), an ancient clapper bridge built across the River Leach in Gloucestershire provides a link between Eastleach Turville to the west and Eastleach Martin to the east. In Norman times these were two manors held by different lords and consequently there was a church to serve each hamlet: St Andrews and St Michael & St Martin. The Keble family were lords of the manor for five generations from the sixteenth century and, immediately after his ordination in 1815, John Keble, author of *The Christian Year*, became non-resident curate of both churches. As well as being a clergyman, Keble was a poet and hymn writer and one of the original members of the Oxford Movement. Keble College Oxford was erected in honour of his memory and to perpetuate his teaching.

The clapper bridge has its roots in prehistoric times and is found in places where suitable materials were most readily available, such as the upland areas of the Pennines and southwest England. Standing over the East Dart river, the clapper bridge at Postbridge on Dartmoor in Devon (above) probably originated in the thirteenth century, at a time when local Cistercian monks were exploiting the wool trade. The clapper bridge at Postbridge is a substantial structure: the huge slabs of stone that form the span are supported by two rectangular drystone piers that stand some 7 feet (2 metres) high in the river. Stone has long been used to form simple river crossings such as stepping stones in shallow water, and causeways across marshland. ❧

Strands of emerald weed are pulled taut by the current as the River Coln flows through the arches of the old Cotswold stone bridge in the village of Bibury in Gloucestershire (right). A ready supply of clear, running water was vital to the cloth industry and these waters once powered a fulling mill. The River Coln itself flows down over the limestone of the Cotswold hills, which take their name from the Saxon words 'cotes', meaning sheepfold, and 'wold', meaning bare hill. The village was once a famous horse-racing centre, and is home to England's oldest racing club. Facing the river from a corner of the churchyard is a large, gabled building, the Bibury Court hotel. The building dates from Tudor times, but the main portion was built in 1633 by Sir Thomas Sackville, whose arms appear over the porch door. Bibury Court was altered in the twentieth century by a cousin of President Roosevelt. ❧

Frampton on Severn stands close to the River Severn, which flows south from Gloucester to reach the Bristol Channel. The village sits in the flat land of the Vale of Berkeley between the head of the estuary and the escarpment of the Cotswold hills. The Gloucester and Sharpness Canal, which links the River Severn with Gloucester, runs close to the mainly fourteenth-century church of St Mary, which lies beside a water meadow somewhat apart from the rest of the village.

The houses at Frampton are a mixture of Georgian brick, timber-frame and cottages with gables and thatched roofs. They stand well back from Rosamund's Green which, at some 22 acres (9 hectares), is one of the largest in England. It takes its name from 'Fair Rosamond', the pet name for Henry II's mistress Rosamond Clifford, who was reputedly born in the village and poisoned by Queen Eleanor in 1177.

Frampton Court was built between 1730 and 1733 for an official of the Bristol Customs House, Richard Clutterbuck, probably by the Bristol architect John Strahan. In the grounds of Frampton Court there is a formal rectangular pond beside which is a Gothic-style orangery.

In the village of Allerford in Somerset an ancient packhorse bridge with two high arches stands over the River Aller as it flows down to nearby Bossington Beach in Porlock Bay. Packhorse trains laden with wool and other goods would have crossed on the bridge, while carts and wagons made use of the ford alongside. In the past, smugglers carried their contraband inland from the coast along this route. The village is set against a backdrop of wooded hills where magnificent chestnuts, oaks and silver firs stand. They were planted by the lord of the manor, Thomas Dyke Acland III, of nearby Holnicote in the 1830s. Acland was a great local benefactor and did much to improve the area round about. Most notable amongst these achievements was the erection of the cottages of the neighbouring village of Selworthy. Allerford itself contains a mix of stone and rendered cottages, some of which date back to the seventeenth century. ❧

Reflected in the waters of the River Cuckmere is Alfriston's church of St Andrew (left), which was built on an ancient Anglo-Saxon burial mound. The village stands where a ridgeway used by prehistoric man descends to cross the river and, in the small square, there is the stump of a medieval market cross. Set in the downland of East Sussex, the river meanders south from the village through water meadows to join the sea less than 4 miles (6 kilometres) away at Cuckmere Haven.

Southeast England was particularly attractive to eighteenth-century smugglers because of its proximity to the Continent, and here, where the chalk of the South Downs is broken by the river valley, much contraband was landed. The distribution of goods often took place at public houses such as Alfriston's timber-framed Star Inn (above) which, dating from around 1420, is said to be one of the oldest in England. It is claimed that the pub was built and maintained by the monks of nearby Battle Abbey.

The Clergy House at Alfriston overlooks the East Sussex downland of the Cuckmere Valley. Probably built as a yeoman farmer's house around 1350, it had passed into the possession of nearby Michelham Priory by 1400. Despite its name, it was probably never the home of a clergyman; it is more likely that the income from it augmented the vicar's stipend. In 1889, however, when the house was threatened with demolition, it was the local vicar who, after a long struggle to raise funds to save it, sought the assistance of the Society for the Protection of Ancient Buildings. The Society brought the Clergy House to the attention of the newly formed National Trust and, once a public appeal had raised the £350 needed to save the building, supervised the work. It was the first property purchased by the Trust – for the princely sum of £10 – and was in a sorry state, with rain streaming through the thatched roof to the rooms below. The staircase had entirely disappeared and its walls bulged ominously. It is said that 'it stood a forlorn relic', in marked contrast to its appearance today.

The wooded gorge on the River Caldew known as the 'Howk' has been hollowed out of the limestone. It lies about a mile above the loosely grouped stone cottages of the village of Caldbeck at the northern end of the Lake District National Park. The clear water of the stream was used by the local brewery and it also powered mills, including a nineteenth-century bobbin mill.

In 1780 nearly 1,800 people lived at Cald-beck, including one John Peel who eloped to Gretna Green with Mary White and went on to father thirteen children. He had a passion for hunting and died in 1854 after falling from his horse. His highly decorated headstone bears hunting horns and, opposite the churchyard gate, there is a sandstone shelter dedicated to him and to John Woodcock Graves, who wrote the words of the song that immortalised his exploits, 'D'ye ken John Peel'. ❧

When St Paulinus came to the Lancashire village of Whalley in AD 626-7, he used the waters of the River Calder to baptise new converts, and three Celtic crosses can still be seen in the churchyard of St Mary's. Today the Calder Valley is dominated by an example of man's ingenuity in conquering the natural landscape: in 1850 a viaduct of forty-nine arches was opened to carry the railway. Such structures were necessary where it was impossible for railway engineers to follow the landscape by means of embankments and cuttings. Seventeen viaducts were built in the 72 miles (116 kilometres) between Carlisle and Settle. In the care of English Heritage is the outer gatehouse of the nearby Whalley Abbey, which flourished from 1300 until the Dissolution of the Monasteries in the 1530s. When it began to be demolished around 1660, much of the stone ended up in local buildings.

Upper Slaughter has the same unity that exists in many other Cotswold villages because of the stone used in the buildings. This was taken from quarries that existed across the parish. By the churchyard is an open square in which there is a group of eight cottages which were remodelled around 1906 by the architect Sir Edwin Lutyens. On a mound to the west of the river there once stood a Norman castle, and excavations in 1961 revealed pottery of the eleventh, twelfth and thirteenth centuries. The church of St Peter also has Norman origins, but was substantially restored in 1877. There are many other fine buildings, including the Old Manor House, which was built by the Slaughter family during the sixteenth century. ⅔

The honey-coloured villages of Upper Slaughter (left) and Lower Slaughter (right) are just a short stroll apart in the rolling Cotswold countryside of Gloucestershire. Through them both run the waters of the River Eye, a tributary of the River Windrush. The name shared by the villages and the Slaughter family does not refer to some ancient and bloody battle, but comes from the Anglo-Saxon meaning 'muddy place'. There is strong evidence that Neolithic people inhabited the area, as thousands of flint leaf-arrowheads have been discovered in the countryside between the Slaughters and Stow-on-the-Wold 3 miles 5 kilometres to the northeast. The appeal of such verdant places to early settlers was no doubt due, at least in part, to the supply of fresh, running water offered by the River Eye.

A simple bridge of wooden planks straddles the broad, shallow stream as it flows through the centre of the village of Lower Slaughter (right) on its journey to meet the River Windrush to the south. Wider here than upstream, the river valley was created by the meltwaters of the thawing ice-sheets at the end of the last Ice Age. Unusually, the banks of the river are neatly lined with stone where they pass in front of the cottages. Indeed, stone is everywhere and has been used for the walls and roofs of the majority of the cottages, some of which date from the late sixteenth or early seventeenth century and are of a style reflected across the Cotswolds.

The tall red-brick chimney of Lower Slaughter's nineteenth-century corn mill (above left) rises above the stone roofs at one end of this village panorama. Its water wheel was powered by the river and continued to operate well into the 1960s.

Many cottages were built with materials and land provided by the landlord, but the tenant supplied the labour. In return, the tenant, his son and his grandson could live rent free, after which time ownership of the cottage reverted to the landlord or his descendants. ❧

The villagers of Lower Slaughter built their homes from the same Cotswold stone that was loaded onto small barges and floated down the River Windrush to the Thames for use in the colleges of Oxford.

Wickhambreaux lies on a tributary of the River Stour in Kent, and its six-storey weather-boarded water mill stands on a site recorded in the Domesday Book of 1086. The power of the river drove all the machinery in the mill, not just the mill stones themselves. The water wheel was connected via a series of wooden- or iron-cogged wheels, and the gearing was arranged so that the stones turned ten to fifteen times faster than the wheel itself.

The fourteenth-century church of St Andrew was altered and restored in the nineteenth century. The Art Nouveau east window was donated by Count James Gallantin of New York. It dates from 1896 and is by Arild Rosencrantz, the first American glassworker to decorate an English church. To the north of Wickhambreaux on the River Stour is Stodmarsh, a rich area of open water and reedbeds.

The bridge at West Tanfield in North York-shire was probably built around 1734, and carries the Ripon road over the River Ure. Bridge design was slow to change, and the typical medieval bridge, with low brick arches of varying spans and a humped and narrow carriageway, continued in many places well into the eighteenth century. The condition of Eng-land's roads and bridges was poor, with many older bridges in a state of steady deterioration, because both their building and upkeep relied on a combination of local subscription, tolls, and the generosity of wealthy individuals, guilds and corporations.

The volume of wheeled traffic increased during the late seventeenth century, and it was alongside the development of turnpike roads that bridge-building boomed. Bridges that were capable of carrying far greater loads began to be constructed, and their design increasingly came to reflect the style of the period. It was not, however, until the early nineteenth century that responsibility for the maintenance of bridges passed to county authorities. ❧

A well-dressing ceremony is held annually on Ascension Day at Bisley in Gloucestershire. The custom was begun in 1863 by the vicar, Thomas Keble, after he had the seven gabled water chutes (above) restored.

In pre-Christian times offerings were made to nymphs to ensure a good supply of water, and fountains, springs and wells were revered. Such sites were often rededicated later to Christian saints. Some wells are known as wishing wells, and many 'holy wells' are claimed to possess therapeutic properties. Well dressing is particularly prevalent in the county of Derbyshire, where children and adults use flowers and leaves to create representations of biblical scenes.

The history of the Somerset village of Chewton Mendip dates back to at least the ninth century, as it was mentioned in King Alfred's will. In those days, goods were transported on the backs of ponies. Merchants and traders relied on their animals to carry all kinds of items across terrain that would defeat any form of wheeled transport. Over time, these packhorse routes became more defined and eventually formed the basis of our modern road network. The oldest surviving packhorse bridges date from the fourteenth century, but they were still being built in the early nineteenth century. Most were wide enough to allow the passage of only one animal, and originally had no parapets because these would have obstructed the panniers that were slung across the animals' backs to distribute the load. All types of goods were carried, including coal or iron ore, wool and building materials. As trade developed, long packhorse trains of twenty or more ponies would travel in single file, with the lead animal wearing a bell that would warn travellers of the train's approach. ❧

According to its inscription, St James's Well at Abinger Common in Surrey 'was built by William John Evelyn Lord of the Manor of Abinger' and was 'declared open for the use of Abinger Parishioners August 11th 1895'. The canopied St James's Well derives its name from the parish church and was built when the land was being developed. A water diviner was employed, who had a reputation for predicting not only almost the exact location, but also the depth of underground water: the well at Abinger is 150 feet (45 metres) deep. Many wells were lost or filled in when they fell out of use and became a danger to animals and children. Other wells, especially those close to cesspools or privies, were abandoned when they became contaminated and carried the risk of spreading typhoid or cholera. 🌿

The River Bain is claimed to be the shortest river in England. Running the 2 miles (3 kilometres) from Semer Water, Yorkshire's largest natural expanse of natural water, it cascades dramatically over the weirs in the Wensleydale village of Bainbridge before joining the River Ure. Unusually for a village, Bainbridge has a long recorded history. In 1227, 'one Ranulph son of Robert' stated that his forbears had founded the village in the Forest of Wensleydale and had provided homes and 9 acres (3.5 hectares) of land for twelve foresters.

In the seventeenth century, during the reign of Charles II, the villagers purchased the manorial rights from the City of London. An early Quaker village, it stands round a spacious village green at the foot of a glacial mound or drumlin called Brough Hill. This was formerly crowned by a Roman military outpost, and a Roman road runs close by to the southwest.

On winter evenings, three blasts on a horn are sounded, a reminder of the ancient custom that helped foresters or shepherds find their way back to the village.

The Shropshire Union Canal passes along the edge of the village of Christleton in Cheshire. Originally known as the Chester Canal, it was begun after the necessary Act of Parliament was obtained in 1772. By 1779 it had connected the River Dee in Chester with Nantwich some 18 miles (29 kilometres) to the east at a cost of around £71,000.

The boatmen working on the canal, or 'the cut' as they called it, took great pride in their narrow boats, often painting them in bright colours. Generally a mere 7 feet (2 metres) wide, a narrow boat will fit almost exactly into the majority of locks on the canal system. Before the narrow boats were equipped with diesel engines, they were hauled by a horse, mule or donkey walking along the towpaths.

Canals became redundant as arteries of trade with the coming of the railways, but many have been saved and are used by pleasure traffic.

On the right, an unusual pillar sundial stands in front of the Manor House. ❧

INDUSTRIAL VILLAGES

ABINGER HAMMER, SURREY • BIBURY, GLOUCESTERSHIRE
CHEWTON MENDIP, SOMERSET • CHIDDINGFOLD, SURREY
CLEY NEXT THE SEA, NORFOLK • FINCHINGFIELD, ESSEX
FRIDAY STREET, SURREY • KERSEY, SUFFOLK • LAVENHAM, SUFFOLK
LONGNOR, STAFFORDSHIRE • THAXTED, ESSEX • TURTON, LANCASHIRE
WICKHAMBREAUX, KENT • WILDBOARCLOUGH, CHESHIRE

VILLAGE STREETS today are beloved for their well-kept buildings, gardens and their quiet romance, but all this belies the activity that would, in the past, have occupied the villagers. Once, the sound of hammering and clanking would have come from workshops at the roadside and cottages hidden away down cobbled alleys, as men and women toiled to produce a huge range of goods.

In the days before mass-production and standardisation, the products of each village had distinct regional styles that depended on locally available raw materials, tradition and the needs of the community. A large degree of self-sufficiency was essential in the production of such workshop items as furniture and cooking utensils, and even those villagers not directly employed on the land frequently kept pigs or hens for food. Further requirements of daily life were provided by cottage industries such as basket-making, spinning, weaving and the making of candles and rush-lights. Woodland crafts needed the simplest of tools, and wattle hurdles of hazel, walking sticks of ash or chestnut and besom brooms made from birch twigs were amongst the items produced.

There was a proud, jealously guarded tradition of apprenticeship, with one generation passing its skills and tools down to the next. Many skilled craftsmen were nonetheless required to be jacks-of-all-trades, mending machinery one day and making fine items the next. As well as acting as builder, the local carpenter might be called upon to repair agricultural implements, build coffins and act as undertaker.

The horse was of supreme importance as a provider of power and transport before the Industrial Revolution, and the glow of the forge, the ring of hammer on anvil and the sight of horses being shod were familiar elements in village life. The smith was both a blacksmith, who worked with iron to produce all manner of items, and a farrier who specialised in shoeing horses. His role as farrier extended to that of equine expert, while his job as blacksmith included the manufacture of nails, hinges, farming tools and equipment, as well as their maintenance.

Some smiths were also wheelwrights or, if not, would work closely with them. In the age before pneumatic tyres, the making of large, spoked wagon wheels was an important and highly skilled job. Made from seasoned elm, oak, ash and beech, the wheels had to be strong enough to carry a fully laden wagon over uneven road surfaces. The tyres were generally made of a continuous iron circle or hoop, which was fitted round the wooden wheel while still hot.

Other than the horse, water and wind were the prime sources of power until well into the eighteenth century. Water wheels date from Roman times, while the windmill did not develop until around 1185. During the Middle Ages, windmills were mainly used for 'fulling' cloth, draining land and grinding corn.

Most parishes had a corn mill and milling was frequently controlled by the customary law of 'mill soke', which was exercised by the lord of the manor. Manorial custom required that the villagers pay a toll for their corn to be ground, which was usually one-sixteenth of the flour produced. Millers were rarely popular figures, for they were often accused of taking more than they were entitled to, and eventually the practice of mill soke changed so that the miller bought the grain from the villagers and sold the flour himself. As a result, mills were enlarged to provide extra storage.

The work of the miller was physically demanding and skilled. He not only had to heave heavy sacks of grain and flour, but also had to maintain the mill's mechanism. In the case of windmills, which depended on the vagaries of the weather, the miller had to work whenever the wind blew, even if this was during the night.

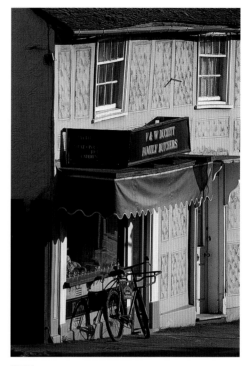

Family-run shops like this butcher's in Thaxted in Essex were once a common sight. Sadly, many village shops have been forced to close because of competition from supermarkets.

Much of England was originally covered by forest but, as the needs of the population increased, the wood was exploited for a diverse range of purposes such as house-building, the production of numerous domestic and industrial implements, the construction of wagons and carts, ship-building, firewood and the production of charcoal.

Charcoal was once vital to such industries as glass- and iron-making because it gives out about twice the heat of an equivalent weight of wood. It is produced by burning wood very slowly in pyres or kilns that are covered with clay and herbage to keep out the air. While the wood is burning, the kilns have to be watched night and day, so generations of charcoal-burners lived in the forests with their families in small camps away from the villages.

Some trees were carefully selected and felled by foresters and, if necessary, the timber was 'seasoned', or left to dry out. To produce beams and planks for house- and ship-building, the great trunks were suspended over a narrow saw-pit and a long saw was pulled rhythmically between one 'sawyer' in the pit and another at ground level.

Iron was smelted in woodland areas that stretched from the Lake District in the north to the Sussex Weald in the south. Access to both plentiful supplies of wood and a fast-flowing stream determined the site: wood provided the charcoal to fuel the blast furnaces and water power drove the bellows and worked the large forges that lifted the hammers.

The extractive industries such as the mining of coal, lead, tin and copper, as well as stone-quarrying, provided work for villagers that was both tough and dangerous. Blasting with gunpowder is said to have begun in copper mines in the 1670s and the production of this explosive substance eventually spread from southeast England to other parts of the country. The ingredients of gunpowder are charcoal, sulphur and saltpetre, which is made from earth, lime, ashes and animal dung or bird droppings. The process of mixing these substances so that they were of a uniform consistency could be dangerous, and accidental explosions were common.

While the remnants of some gunpowder works still stand in the countryside, the land is also pock-marked by another industry, although it is easy to miss the signs. Where clay is present, dips and irregular ground can indicate the location of a 'brick field', a rather grand name for what might be a small area dug to supply the needs of just one building. Clay was dug up and left to break down through the action of frost. In the spring it was mixed with other ingredients, such as sand, lime and clinker (slag), and ground in a pug mill before being thrown into a wooden mould, allowed to dry slowly and then fired in a kiln.

From the early Middle Ages, the wool industry brought great wealth to some parts of England as huge quantities were exported to Europe. The woolpack was the symbol of the trade and, in the fourteenth century, Edward III ordered that the Lord Chancellor sit on a woolsack in the House of Lords in recognition of the pre-eminence of the wool industry – a tradition that continues to this day.

Cloth-making constituted a major cottage industry in almost every county where sheep were reared. As there were so many processes involved in the manufacture of cloth, entrepreneurs would frequently purchase wool from farmers and subcontract the various stages of work to small family units.

Most cloth needed to be cleaned and thickened by 'fulling', which was done by soaking the cloth in a mixture of fuller's earth and various cleansers, such as wood ash. Originally, the cloth was trodden in small tubs or pits but, by the late twelfth century, the process had been mechanised and human feet were replaced by wooden, water-powered hammers in fulling mills. After fulling, the piece of cloth was stretched on a tenter-frame or rack so that it would dry evenly and not become misshapen.

Wool was not the only material worked in English villages. Some communities specialised in silk weaving; in others, hemp and flax were grown to be spun and woven into sacks or sheets for domestic use, as well as for ropes. Gloves were made in many villages in Worcestershire and lace was worked in Buckinghamshire and Devon.

Lace-workers worked in their cottages by the light of a lamp or candle that shone through a glass globe filled with water and aqua fortis (nitric acid) to magnify the light. When the weather was suitable the workers would often sit at the doorway to make maximum use of daylight. For those engaged in cottage industry, it was far from the romantic life one might imagine, and often involved insanitary conditions and long hours of eye-straining work. Unlike the craftsmen of the city guilds, who were strictly regulated, village workers were not organised and could not demand good wages and conditions. As a result, village workers were frequently exploited by unscrupulous employers.

Many river-side villages had water mills like this one at Wickhambreaux in Kent. Like windmills, many water mills have fallen into disrepair or been destroyed.

With the coming of the second half of the eighteenth century, the traditional, self-sufficient way of village life began to change. The Industrial Revolution was unstoppable and, with the agricultural labour force already considerably reduced because of mechanisation and changing farming practices, the working population moved from the land to the expanding towns.

As the transport of goods via the great arteries of the new canals and railways became easier, so cheap, mass-produced products became widely available and the industrial map changed for ever. New skills, production methods and materials were developed. Meanwhile, cottage industries such as cloth manufacture became factory-based in a process that was inexorable and which saw the birth of an urban class that was divorced from the land and the ways of the village.

In medieval times Cley next the Sea was a prosperous and important port on the north Norfolk coast at the mouth of the River Glaven. Large quantities of grain and wool were exported from here and ships also came to wharves farther up the river to collect flour from a post mill (see page 168). In the early seventeenth century, land reclamation caused the Glaven to silt up and the village now stands about 1 mile (1.5 kilometres) inland from its beach. Overlooking salt marshes and nearby Blakeney harbour from above the remains of an old quay, Cley windmill dates from 1713, although the tower was built later. Steven Barnabus Burroughs was the best-known of the millers and he worked and owned the mill from 1840 to 1919, after which it fell into disrepair. In 1921 it was converted into holiday accommodation.

The village's former glory is reflected in the size of nearby St Margaret's church, which contains interesting carvings and brasses. ❦

The medieval church of St John the Baptist, which dominates Thaxted, was built by the de Clare family, who owned the manor. In the fourteenth and fifteenth centuries Thaxted was probably the most prosperous place in Essex, and records show that in 1381 there were seventy-nine cutlers, eleven smiths and two goldsmiths. This prosperity was reflected in the church. The timber-framed guildhall (right) was built in the fifteenth century by the Cutlers' Guild as a meeting place and market hall. Although the cutlery industry declined in the sixteenth century, Thaxted was established as a market centre by 1686. The windmill (above), which was built in 1804, stands on the site of an earlier mill above a double row of almshouses: homes provided by charitable foundations for the poor, elderly and infirm. ❧

The white weather-boarded windmill in Finchingfield in Essex was purchased by the community and restored in 1949. Such mills are known as post mills and were the earliest type of windmill. A central post supported the whole structure, which could be rotated by means of a tail pole or tiller beam. This allowed the miller to turn the sails into the wind. A hoist was used to lift the full sacks of grain to the top floor where it was stored in bins. It was then released to the middle floor to be ground between millstones that were turned by a system of gears driven by the sails. The resulting flour passed down to the ground floor and was collected in bags.

Windmills have been called 'landships' because the wooden structure creaked and moved like a great sailing vessel and the miller had to be as vigilant as any sea captain. Early sails were covered with sailcloth and had to be adjusted by hand, but around 1770 spring sails were introduced with shutters that were regulated by the wind.

The Cheshire village of Wildboarclough, once known as Crag, sits under the sharp peak of Shutlingsloe close to the western edge of the Peak District National Park. With its row of cottages displaying their Gothic-style windows, an inn and a church, the village has great charm. The small church of St Saviour was consecrated in 1909, having been built by the local landowner, the sixteenth Earl of Derby, in thanks for the return of his sons from the South African War. It is Crag Mill, however, that marks Wildboarclough's place in industrial history, producing silk and, it is said, cotton and carpets for the Great Exhibition of 1851. This exhibition of contemporary developments in manufacturing, design and industry was housed in Joseph Paxton's Crystal Palace in London's Hyde Park. For many ordinary people of the day, a visit to the exhibition was also their first trip to the capital city. Many experienced their first railway journey to see the technology that was changing the village way of life for ever. 🬼

In the Middle Ages the name of the Suffolk village of Kersey was known far and wide for the coarse, hard-wearing cloth of twill weave produced there, which was worn throughout Europe as well as by the tradesmen and yeomen of England. During the fourteenth century, a small colony of Flemish cloth-workers had settled in the village and used the tributary of the River Brett, which cuts across The Street, to soak newly made cloth. The cloth was produced as 'pieces' which, less than a yard (1 metre) wide, were originally of some 16 to 18 yards (15 to 16 metres) in length but, by the eighteenth century, were often over 40 yards (37 metres) long. Large quantities of this cloth were exported to be made into overcoats and army uniforms.

The quality and size of the church of St Mary, which stands impressively on a rise above Kersey, gives a good indication of the village's past importance. A group of wonderful timber-framed weavers' cottages has survived in The Street, and other colour-washed houses lead down to the ford. ❧

Etched with lichens and mosses, the steeply pitched and undulating roofs of the cottages of Arlington Row, at Bibury in Gloucestershire, blend so perfectly with their surroundings that they give the impression of having been hewn from the landscape. The long, curving terrace probably originated as a fourteenth-century sheephouse or wool store. In the early seventeenth century it was converted to house the weavers who supplied cloth for the nearby Arlington Mill. Secured for the nation by the National Trust, Arlington Row stands by a four-acre field known as Rack Isle, which is bounded by water on three sides, and which owes its name to the fact that it was here that wool was hung on racks to dry.

Wool was produced in substantial quantities in the area as long ago as the Roman occupation. By the time the Domesday Book was compiled in 1086, the power of the River Coln, which passes through the village, was already harnessed. A new mill was built on the site around 1650 to serve the dual role of fulling cloth and grinding corn. The Cotswold hills, because of their thin soil, offer ideal pasturage for sheep. English and particularly Cotswold wool was prized throughout medieval Europe, and merchants from Italy and Flanders came to buy it in great quantities. ❧

William Morris, the Victorian artist, writer and craftsman, thought Bibury the 'prettiest village in England'. All the typical characteristics are here: neat mullioned windows below a dripstone, miniature dormer windows peeking out from stone-clad roofs, and doors with straight-headed lintels.

Stone dominates at Bibury, not just in the cottages of Arlington Row (right), but in what has been described as 'perhaps the most enchanting churchyard in England'. Here Georgian and Victorian masons were able to take full advantage of the qualities of the local limestone by carving it exquisitely. Cherub heads look out from the ends of table tombs, some of which have double-roll tops; gravestones with an intricate tracery of rococo motifs lean at angles in the spacious green sward as if basking in the afternoon sun. St Mary's church stands at the northern end of the village, overlooking a square of stone houses. Although the church is Saxon in origin, it has had many later additions and alterations. ❧

One of the greatest of all the East Anglian 'wool churches', St Peter and St Paul was built on Lavenham's prosperity as a centre of the Suffolk wool trade between the fourteenth and sixteenth centuries. The arms, emblems and merchant marks of the great clothiers of Lavenham appear throughout the church because it was their money that made its construction possible. Chief amongst these benefactors were the Spring family and the Lord of the Manor, John de Vere, the 13th Earl of Oxford. Records show that work on the tower was underway around 1486 and that, in 1523, Thomas Spring III left what was then the considerable sum of £200 to complete it and also to build a chapel as a monument to himself and his wife. ᕙ

Staffordshire is well known for its coalfields and potteries, yet in 1951 it became home to part of Britain's first National Park: the Peak District National Park. The village of Longnor is perched high on the gritstone moors at the southern end of the park and has robust, unspoilt gritstone buildings. Just to the east of the village centre, and forming the county border with Derbyshire, flows the River Dove. In this pastoral environment, agriculture and

especially dairy farming predominate. Small field barns provide shelter for cattle in hard weather, where they are fed with hay from an overhead loft. Longnor was once a major cheese-making area, made prosperous through its fairs and markets. During the Second World War all farmhouse cheese-making was stopped and, sadly, after the war few small-scale cheese-makers resumed business.

Humphrey Chetham was born in Manchester in 1580. He became a merchant and cloth manufacturer, founded the Chetham Library in Manchester and acquired Turton Tower in Lancashire near to the village of Turton. Here, in the valley of the River Bradshaw, the village pub bears his name, as does Chetham Farm Cottage (above).

Cotton was first introduced into East Anglia from the eastern Mediterranean and had reached Lancashire by 1600. Like many villages, Turton was directly affected by the Industrial Revolution and particularly by the development of the cotton industry in the late eighteenth century at nearby Bolton, which became a major manufacturing town. Merchants and manufacturers in the town became rich and some chose to live in surrounding villages such as Turton. ✻

Amongst the tile-hung houses at Abinger Hammer in Surrey, the Victorian clock is a prominent landmark. The figure of a man striking a bell is a reminder of the time when this part of the now-quiet valley of the River Tillingbourne rang to the sounds of the iron industry: the clank of mechanical hammers, the wheeze of bellows and the churning of water wheels. Before the Industrial Revolution, iron-working was an important industry in Surrey and right across that area of southern England known as the Weald.

At nearby Friday Street (left) a few cottages and a pub huddle together beside a wide hammer pond. This pond was created in the late sixteenth century by damming one of the streams feeding the Tillingbourne. The water was used to drive mill wheels which in turn operated the heavy hammers in local iron works. ❧

A former lead-mining village, Chewton
Mendip stands at the source of the River
Chew on the slopes of the Mendip Hills in
Somerset. Over the centuries lead has been
exploited extensively in the production of gun
shot, paints, pottery glazes and crystal glass. The
Romans were attracted to lead-mining because
of the quantity of silver that could be extracted
from the metal. The Saxons used lead for roofing, and many churches of all sizes are clad with
large areas of sheet lead. It has been used to
make water pipes, gutters, water cisterns, elaborate hopper heads on down pipes, and to form
the 'cames' which hold small pieces of window
glass together. England and Spain once supplied
the bulk of the world's lead and from 1750 to
1850 over a million tons were produced in
Britain alone.

In the parish church at Chiddingfold in Surrey is a small stained-glass window made from 427 fragments of glass. What is unusual is that these pieces were found locally, near the sites of glass furnaces. The window is dedicated to the 'memory of Chiddingfold glassmakers and others connected with the industry for a period of at least four hundred years'. The village is said to have been the centre of English glassmaking and, in its heyday, it provided glass for the royal chapels in Westminster Abbey and Windsor Castle. The industry was probably begun by Frenchmen who came to Surrey and Sussex around the beginning of the thirteenth century. The glassmakers established furnaces in places that today bear names such as Glasshouse Copse and Glasshouse Field. The glasshouses were oblong buildings that contained furnaces, and were nearly always built at the top of a slope to catch the breeze.

COASTAL VILLAGES

BLAKENEY, NORFOLK • BOSHAM, WEST SUSSEX • CLOVELLY, DEVON
LYNMOUTH, DEVON • POLPERRO, CORNWALL • PORLOCK WEIR, SOMERSET
PORTLOE, CORNWALL • STAITHES, NORTH YORKSHIRE

ENGLAND HAS SOME TWO THOUSAND MILES (over three thousand kilometres) of coastline broken only by the Welsh Marches to the west and the border with Scotland to the north. The underlying geology has given this coastline a marvellous variety, which ranges from majestic cliffs and rocky promontories to long curving beaches and gently sloping coves.

A wonderful diversity of materials goes to form this landscape. Granite, limestone and sandstone contribute to a palette of colours that range from black through blood red, pink, grey, golden brown and green to dazzling white. These ancient stones are revealed in everything from dunes of the finest sands to towering cliffs, from pebbles graded by the sand to boulders strewn as though dropped by a giant hand.

The map is constantly changing as the sea nibbles away at earth and rock and creates new sand bars to trap the unwary sailor. Much has been done over the centuries to try to stop this encroachment. As far back as Roman times, local people built dykes and embankments to drain marshland for agricultural use. In the intervening years, the sea has reclaimed entire villages. Elsewhere, man-made sea defences, such as harbours hewn from local stone and breakwaters formed of great baulks of timber, seem to draw the village down to the water, adding a charm and ruggedness to the scene.

No coastal village can fail to be affected by the sea: its moods and ever-changing rhythms are constantly there, tranquil one minute and menacing the next. The light is different here too, with a brightness and shimmering clarity all of its own. A salty tang in the air and the unmistakable sound of the sea tumbling over the shore complete the scene.

Village buildings are traditionally wrought from local materials and, as a result, often seem to meld into their surroundings. Winding cobbled lanes plunge down hills to tiny harbours where colour-washed cottages and bright fishing boats are reflected in the water. Fishermen's simple timber huts look careworn as their protective covering of paint or tar becomes bleached and blistered by the constant presence of salt in the air. Even the grander buildings need constant attention if they are to retain their elegance and survive the battering of the bracing winds that are capable of knocking the breath from one's body.

The English coast was once an important highway for trade and raw materials since boats provided a much cheaper and quicker method of transport than the packhorse trains and wagons that travelled overland. Long detours were worthwhile as boats could carry much greater loads and could sail up rivers to inland communities. In the eighteenth century, many villages lost their trade when creeks and inlets silted up. Later, ships that plied coastal waters needed deep-water anchorage that was unavailable in many small harbours. Coastal paths that once provided the main route between one village and another now offer spectacular clifftop walks for ramblers.

Everything from coal to cheese passed along the coast, but it was not just this legal trade that engaged the coastal population. Smuggling proved equally rewarding for many communities and, despite severe penalties, was regarded by the majority of the public as a relatively innocent occupation. The highly organised smugglers were divided into two distinct groups: seamen who specialised in handling vessels that sailed close enough to the shore to land the contraband, and the landsmen who organised its storage and assisted in its distribution. Along some parts of the coast, practically every resident was said to be involved in the trade, and houses were connected by passages and cellars to enable the 'invisible' movement of smuggled goods.

With the public and many officials, even if not directly involved, certainly turning a blind eye, the authorities could do little to combat the trade. However, pitched battles between the smugglers and the king's men were not unknown.

At the end of the sixteenth century French, Flemish and English ships were running the gauntlet of the revenue men by smuggling tobacco into Cornwall, and it was not long before spirits, sugar and tea were added to the list. However, it was with the Napoleonic wars of the early nineteenth century and the imposition of heavy duties on imported wines, spirits and other goods, especially those from France, that smuggling flourished.

The war against France meant that the navy's need for fighting men became urgent and press-gangs went to work. These military or naval detachments would frequently ply an unwary subject with drink, then press money on him. Once a man had accepted the 'king's shilling' he was required to serve the Crown for as long as his assigned ship was in service. The press-gang often carried heavy clubs to deal with men who would not come willingly, although extreme violence was rare as the courts dealt severely with press officers who killed or injured men. In theory, only seafaring men could be pressed, but in practice any

Staithes in North Yorkshire was an early home to the explorer Captain James Cook. He lodged in a cottage on the harbour when, at the age of thirteen, he served as a shopkeeper's apprentice.

able-bodied man was a target. Such were the numbers of fishermen and merchantmen being taken that the effect was felt on trade and, in 1801, a statute was introduced to exempt fishermen from falling victim to press-gangs.

Fish had long been a vital part of the diet for those living on the coast, but it was not until the coming of the railways in the 1840s that fresh fish could be transported inland fast enough to arrive in a palatable condition. Previously the only fish available had been smoked and salted or air-dried to preserve it.

Not only did the railways transform the fishing industry, they also turned the seaside into a place to visit. Villagers found work serving nearby resorts and there were fresh opportuni-

Built on a peninsula that juts out into an inlet of Chichester harbour, Bosham is typical of villages that stand on a tidal creek. Many cottages on the harbour road are approached by steps, which prevent flood water from entering the buildings.

ties to sell their goods and produce to day-trippers. The railways also played a part in giving many of the younger generation a chance to move away from the villages into towns: by 1901, almost seventy percent of Britain's thirty-seven million inhabitants had become urban dwellers. The fishing industry that was once the mainstay of many coastal communities has dwindled dramatically in recent years and, although some smaller fleets survive, fishing boats are a rare sight in many villages and one is more likely to see a few abandoned lobster pots than bustling activity.

In village churchyards one finds the graves of sailors drowned when their ships went down in gales. Today the heavy thud of the maroon calling the lifeboat crew to action is a reminder that the sea is still a merciless place. Over four hundred lifeboatmen and women have lost their lives since the establishment of the Royal National Lifeboat Institution in 1824. The lighthouses that dot the coast warn of danger and act as beacons to those at sea. They are built to resist the harshest wind and waves, and their construction has sometimes involved great ingenuity and skill. Every lighthouse has a unique history. The Romans built a number of lighthouses in England, including two at Dover. During the Middle Ages, lights were shown from church buildings and were sometimes tended by hermits. In 1514, Henry VIII granted the Corporation of Trinity House a Royal Charter giving them general powers to regulate pilotage. In 1566 Henry's daughter, Elizabeth I, passed an Act of Parliament giving the Corporation the powers to erect seamarks, such as beacons, buoys and other aids to navigation which made the lives of fisherman and other seafarers considerably safer.

Flint and brick cottages stand in the high street that leads to the quay at Blakeney in Norfolk. A Carmelite friary was founded here in 1296 and the village contains a fine medieval guildhall.

In the past, shipwrecks brought rich pickings. Those living along the coast considered the contents of shipwrecks fair game and the practice of scavenging goods from wrecked vessels was widespread in the eighteenth and nineteenth centuries. In 1784, a ship called the *Hope of Amsterdam* was wrecked in Deadman's Bay on Chesil Beach on the south coast. The ship was carrying a cargo of £50,000 in gold, and wild scenes went on for ten days as crowds thronged the beach, fighting for their share. There are also dark tales of villagers in some parts of the country deliberately wrecking ships by luring them onto the rocks.

A less sinister harvest from the sea was seaweed, or 'wrack'. In the winter, storms threw wrack onto the seashore which was collected for use as fertiliser and taken by cart or packhorse along the wrack roads that led from the beaches. Because seaweed is such a rich fertiliser, it is still collected today for use on coastal farms, where it is spread onto the ground and then ploughed in to enrich the soil.

Overlooking Veryan Bay on Cornwall's south coast is the fishing village of Portloe. The tranquillity of the tiny harbour is shattered in stormy weather when it becomes impossible for the fishing boats to navigate between the rocks.

Myths and legends play a large part in the history of the area. It is said that in the fifth century the body of Gerennius, a king of Cornwall, was rowed across nearby Gerrans Bay. The voyage was made in a golden boat with silver oars and the king was buried beneath Carne Beacon, which stands inland to the west of Portloe.

Veryan Bay and the cliffs surrounding it are owned by the National Trust. Veryan itself sits inland of Portloe in a sheltered, wooded dell where roundhouses guard the main entrances to the village. The roundhouses have Gothic-style windows and thatched roofs topped by crosses and, according to local folklore, each was built by a parson for one of his daughters. Their circular shape was designed to deter the devil since, without corners, there is nowhere for him to hide. ❧

The Saxon tower of the church of the Holy Trinity (far left) rises proudly above the village of Bosham. The church is represented in the Bayeux tapestry, for it was here that Harold Godwinson, later King Harold, is said to have prayed in 1064. Two years later, Harold was killed at the Battle of Hastings, defeated by William the Conqueror.

Bosham claims another place in history as the scene of King Canute's legendary attempt to halt the rising tide. Local tradition has it that the king's youngest daughter was buried at the church, a story that was given weight by the discovery, over a hundred years ago, of a Saxon coffin containing the skeleton of a child.

The village itself is an attractive mix of brick and stone houses, many of which are tile-hung. 🪁

Lying on the north Norfolk coast, the extensive salt marshes at Blakeney provide a haven for wildfowl. In the sixteenth and seventeenth centuries the village was a thriving port, although the mudbanks and shallows of the area could make it treacherous. It is said that the twin towers – one large and one small – of the church of St Nicholas acted as beacons to guide the masters of vessels into the harbour. While grain was the major export, Flemish bricks, salt, timber and coal were all landed at Blakeney, and commercial activity continued until the beginning of the twentieth century. Now the estuary has silted up, leaving only a narrow channel. The sand and shingle spit of Blakeney Point is preserved by the National Trust and, as one of Britain's foremost bird sanctuaries, it is a birdwatchers' paradise. Common and grey seals can also be seen. ❧

Set in the cleft of a wooded hillside, Clovelly on the North Devon coast was once a herring fishing village. Like many others on the Devon and Cornish coasts, it developed in the sixteenth century and prospered during the eighteenth and nineteenth centuries. Huddled together, many of the houses are late Georgian, and a combination of whitewash and flowers gives Clovelly a Mediterranean air. Between 1884 and 1936 Christine Hamlyn owned the village, and she is credited with maintaining its character by restoring many of the houses, a number of which display her initials. Today, cars are banned from the village and wooden sleds are used by the locals to carry the necessities of everyday life up and down the steep, cobbled lanes. The church of All Saints stands at the cliff top and has a monument to Charles Kingsley, the nineteenth-century clergyman and author of *Westward Ho!* ❧

olperro is placed like a jewel between jagged rocks and steep wooded hills on the typically rugged yet beautiful Cornish coast-line. It is easy to imagine the night-time flash of a smuggler's lantern here, and it is believed that this was the site of the first station for the 'Pre-ventive Men', or customs and excise officers.

Today, boats still head out into the English Channel from the shelter of the harbour, the entrance to which is so narrow that it can be closed with floating barriers, or 'booms', when the weather is rough.

In Polperro the houses stand right on the sea wall so that, when the tide is in, their reflections mingle with those of the fishing boats on the waters of the lagoon-like harbour. The architecture of Polperro is rugged yet brightly colour-washed and the granite used to construct some of the cottages has been laid without mortar. The oldest surviving house dates from the sixteenth century, while others have elegant yet plain Georgian facades.

Records show that Polperro was a fishing village by the middle of the fourteenth century. By the 1850s, around two-thirds of the villagers were involved in the industry. When the pilchard shoals entered Cornish waters, many local farmers who had finished harvesting their crops would switch to fishing. When the catch was brought ashore it was salted and packed, ready for despatch. ❦

Coastal villages display a wonderful diversity of architecture, and the coloured margin lights of a Polperro porch are enhanced by the typically bright, clear light of the seaside. Cornwall is a Mecca for artists who find inspiration both in the quality of the light and the spectacular scenery. 🦞

The deep gorge of Staithes Beck divides the village of Staithes in two. Nearby is Boulby Cliff which, at 666 feet (200 metres), is the highest point on England's eastern coast. First recorded in 1415, Staithes means 'landing place', and its tall, robust houses dominate the maze of narrow cobbled streets that run between the cliffs. The presence of a lifeboat station testifies to the harsh realities of the North Sea which, all too often, has inundated the village and carried buildings away with it.

In its eighteenth-century heyday, cod, haddock, mackerel and lobster were the staples of life in Staithes. Sadly, the town of Whitby, with its larger harbour further down the coast, captured much of the fishing trade when steam trawlers were introduced. However, there was also a livelihood to be found inland, where potash, alum, ironstone and jet were mined. The black jet stone enjoyed particular popularity during the reign of Queen Victoria, when it was used for mourning jewellery.

Once a herring-fishing village, Lynmouth, on the North Devon coast, is hemmed in by steep, verdant hills and became popular as a place for holidays at the beginning of the nineteenth century. Samuel Taylor Coleridge likened it, and the surrounding area, to Switzerland and the poet Shelley reputedly spent his honeymoon here in 1812, but it was the Victorians who developed Lynmouth by building hotels and villas on the hillside. In 1890, a water-powered railway was built on the esplanade to connect Lynmouth to the cliff-top village of Lynton. Still in service, the two cars are linked by pulleys.Each has a water tank which when filled at the top of the hill drives the car down, thus raising the other. Many buildings in Lynmouth were destroyed on a single night in August 1952 when, after torrential rain, the River Lyn burst its banks, causing a flash flood to sweep through the village, with the result that over thirty people lost their lives.

Boats, such as the one shown above in the harbour at Polperro, have played an important role in England's history. In the past, distinct regional variations in boat design developed to suit local conditions and the task they were intended to perform. The small boats of England enjoyed their biggest triumph during the Second World War, when hundreds of them were mobilised and navigated across the Channel to take part in the rescue of some 335,000 Allied troops at Dunkirk in 1940.

Porlock means 'the enclosure by the harbour', yet the sea has retreated to such an extent that the Somerset village of Porlock stands about 1 mile (1.5 kilometres) inland. Today it is to Porlock Weir, to the west, that one must go to find the pebble banks of a tiny harbour and a cluster of houses. This little port existed in the fifteenth century, and in the early 1800s a quay was created, along with warehouses. Overlooking the Bristol Channel and the coast of Wales beyond, it was once the haunt of smugglers and wreckers. A footpath through the woods leads up to Culbone Church. Dating from Norman times, the church stands 400 feet (120 metres) above sea level, and is said to be the smallest complete medieval church in England. With walls 2 feet (60 cm) thick and a window cut from a solid block of stone, it is only 34 feet (10.5 metres) long and 12 feet (3.7 metres) wide and can seat about thirty people. Inland, straddling both Devon and Somerset, is the great expanse of the Exmoor National Park, where Exmoor ponies and wild red deer wander freely. ❧

1 Hambleden
2 Nether Winchendon
3 Christleton
4 Wildboarclough
5 Luxulyan
6 Polperro
7 Portloe
8 Caldbeck
9 Crosby Garrett
10 Dufton
11 Milburn
12 Morland
13 Hartington
14 Brent Tor
15 Clovelly
16 Lynmouth
17 Postbridge
18 Stoke
19 Widecombe-
   in-the-Moor
20 Romaldkirk
21 Alfriston
22 Finchingfield
23 Thaxted
24 Bibury
25 Bisley
26 Chalford
27 Eastleach
28 Frampton on Severn
29 Lower Slaughter
30 Upper Slaughter
31 Stanton
32 Chawton
33 Selborne
34 Broadway
35 Weobley
36 Much Hadham
37 Wickhambreaux
38 Smarden
39 Ivychurch
40 Turton
41 Whalley

42 Blakeney
43 Cley next the Sea
44 New Buckenham
45 Great Brington
46 Bainbridge
47 Carlton-in-Cleveland
48 Husthwaite
49 Hutton-le-Hole
50 Lastingham
51 Ripley
52 Staithes
53 West Tanfield
54 Laxton
55 Great Tew
56 Kelmscott
57 Tong
58 Allerford
59 Chewton Mendip

60 East Quantoxhead
61 Luccombe
62 Porlock Weir
63 Selworthy
64 Abbots Bromley
65 Longnor
66 Clare

67 Horringer
68 Kersey
69 Lavenham
70 Monks Eleigh
71 Woolpit
72 Abinger Common
73 Abinger Hammer

74 Albury
75 Bletchingley
76 Chiddingfold
77 Friday Street
78 Ockham
79 Shere
80 Witley
81 Amberley
82 Bosham
83 Haworth
84 Castle Combe

210

LIST OF VILLAGES BY COUNTY

The following list includes village events and places to visit in the counties featured in the book, along with directions to the villages photographed. Many village events take place at irregular intervals and at short notice, so check with the relevant Tourist Information Office before you depart.

BUCKINGHAMSHIRE

Annual village events in the county include fêtes and flower festivals as well as garden openings.

Buckingham Tourist Information Centre, The Old Gaol Museum, Market Hill, Buckingham, Bucks MK18 1JX. Tel: (01280) 823020.

HAMBLEDEN
Off the A4155, 3 miles (5 kilometres) northeast of Henley-on-Thames.

NETHER WINCHENDON
Between the A41 and the A418, 5 miles (8 kilometres) west of Aylesbury.

CHESHIRE

Annual events in the county include the Cheshire show, held in Tabley every June.

Chester Visitor Centre, Town Hall, Chester. Tel: (01244) 351609.

CHRISTLETON
Off the A41, 2½ miles (4 kilometres) southeast of Chester.

WILDBOARCLOUGH
Off the A54, 6 miles (10 kilometres) southwest of Buxton.

CORNWALL

Annual events in the county include carnivals and traditional May Day celebrations. Polperro's attractions include a Museum of Smuggling.

Newquay Tourist Information Centre, Marcus Hill, Newquay TR7 1BD. Tel: (01637) 871345.

LUXULYAN
Between the A390 and A391, 4 miles (6 kilometres) north of St Austell.

POLPERRO
On the A387, 5 miles (8 kilometres) west of Looe.

PORTLOE
Off the A3078, 8 miles (13 kilometres) southeast of Truro.

CUMBRIA

Annual events in the county include rushbearing ceremonies and the Biggest Liar in the World Competition. An annual sports show is held in Grasmere every August.

Cumbria Tourist Board, Ashleigh, Holly Road, Windermere, Cumbria LA23 2AQ. Tel: (015394) 44444.

CALDBECK
On the B5229, 11 miles (18 kilometres) southwest of Carlisle.

CROSBY GARRETT
Off the A685, 2½ miles (5 kilometres) west of Kirkby Stephen.

DUFTON
Off the A66, 3 miles (5 kilometres) north of Appleby-in-Westmorland.

MILBURN
Off the A66, 5 miles (8 kilometres) north of Appleby-in-Westmorland.

MORLAND
Off the A66, 5 miles (8 kilometres) west of Appleby-in-Westmorland.

DERBYSHIRE

Annual events in the county include a Shrovetide football match with teams of any number and no rules; well dressing, and a garland ceremony in which a flower-strewn 'king' rides through the street.

Derby Tourist Information Centre, Assembly Rooms, Market Place, Derby DE1 3AH. Tel: (01332) 255802.

HARTINGTON
On the B5054, 9 miles (15 kilometres) southeast of Buxton.

DEVON

Annual events in the county include the Hunting of the Earl of Rone, in Combe Martin, where the 'Earl' rides through the streets on a donkey before being thrown in the sea. Westward Ho! holds a Pot Walloping Festival, in which pebbles are hurled up onto a ridge to mark the end of winter.

West Country Tourist Board, St David's Hill, Exeter, Devon EX4 4SY. Tel: (01392) 425426.

BRENT TOR
This landmark is off the A386, 5 miles (8 kilometres) north of Tavistock.

CLOVELLY
Off the A39, 11 miles (18 kilometres) west of Bideford.

LYNMOUTH
On the A39, 17 miles (27 kilometres) west of Minehead.

POSTBRIDGE
On the B3212, in Dartmoor Forest, 20 miles (32 kilometres) northeast of Plymouth.

STOKE
Off the B3248 and the A39, 15 miles (24 kilometres) west of Bideford.

WIDECOMBE-IN-THE-MOOR
On the B3387, 10 miles (16 kilometres) west of Newton Abbot.

DURHAM

Annual events in the region include the Durham Mustard Tasting Festival and the Durham county show, every July.

Northumbria Tourist Board, Aykley Heads, Durham DH1 5UX. Tel: (0191) 375 3000.

ROMALDKIRK
On the B6277, in the Pennines, 5 miles (8 kilometres) northwest of Barnard Castle.

EAST SUSSEX

Annual events in the county include the Jack-in-the-Green Morris Dance Festival, which incorporates the traditional crowning of the May Queen.

Eastbourne Tourist Information Centre, Cornfield Road, Eastbourne BN21 4QL. Tel: (01323) 411400.

ALFRISTON
Off the A27 and A259, 6 miles (10 kilometres) west of Eastbourne.

ESSEX

Annual events in the county include the Great Dunmow 'flitch of bacon' which is presented to any married couple who can prove not to have had an argument in the past twelve months. A booklet listing events is available each summer from the Chelmsford Tourist Information Office.

Chelmsford Tourist Information Office, County Hall, Chelmsford CM1 1GG. Tel: (01245) 283400.

FINCHINGFIELD
On the B1053 and B1057, 8 miles (13 kilometres) northwest of Braintree.

THAXTED
On the B1051 and the B184, 6 miles (10 kilometres) southeast of Saffron Walden.

GLOUCESTERSHIRE

Annual events in the county include morris dancing, village festivals and flower shows.

Cirencester Tourist Information Centre, Corn Hall, Market Place, Cirencester GK7 2NW. Tel: (01285) 654180.

BIBURY
On the B4225, 7 miles (11 kilometres) northeast of Cirencester.

BISLEY
Between the A419 and B4070, 3 miles (5 kilometres) east of Stroud.

CHALFORD
On the A419, 3 miles (5 kilometres) southeast of Stroud.

EASTLEACH
Between the A361 and the B4425, 12 miles (19 kilometres) east of Cirencester.

FRAMPTON ON SEVERN
Off Junction 13 of the M5, on the B4071, 7 miles (11 kilometres) west of Stroud.

LOWER SLAUGHTER
Between the A429 and the B4068, 3 miles (5 kilometres) southwest of Stow-on-the-Wold.

UPPER SLAUGHTER
Between the A429 and the B4068, 3 miles (5 kilometres) southwest of Stow-on-the-Wold.

STANTON
Off the B4632, 12 miles (19 kilometres) northwest of Cheltenham.

HAMPSHIRE

Annual events in Hampshire include traditional May Day and Guy Fawke's Night celebrations. Jane Austen's House in Chawton is open to the public. Tel: (01420) 83262.

Southern Tourist Board, 40 Chamberlayne Road, Eastleigh, Hampshire SO5 5JH. Tel: (01703) 620006.

CHAWTON
On the A31, 2 miles (3 kilometres) southeast of Alton.

SELBORNE
On the B3006, 4 miles (6 kilometres) southeast of Alton.

HEREFORD AND WORCESTER

Annual events in the county include flower festivals and village fairs, one of which is held regularly in Broadway.

Heart of England Tourist Board, Woodside, Larkhill Road, Worcester WR5 2EZ. Tel: (01905) 763436.

BROADWAY
On the A424 and B4632, 13 miles (21 kilometres) northeast of Cheltenham.

WEOBLEY
On the B4230, off the A44, 8 miles (13 kilometres) southwest of Leominster.

HERTFORDSHIRE

Annual events in the county include duck races, ploughing competitions and 'beating the bounds' ceremonies.

Hertford Tourist Information Centre, 10 Market Place, Hertford SG14 1DG. Tel: (01992) 584322.

MUCH HADHAM
On the B1004, 4½ miles (7 kilometres) west of Bishop's Stortford.

KENT

Annual events in the county include the Rochester Sweeps Festival, made up of a number of traditional ceremonies, such as morris dancing and a sweeps' procession.

South East England Tourist Board, The Old Brew House, Warwick Park, Tunbridge Wells, Kent TN2 5TU. Tel: (01892) 540766.

IVYCHURCH
Off the A2070, 14 miles (22 kilometres) southwest of Hythe.

SMARDEN
Between the A28 and A274, 9 miles (14 kilometres) west of Ashford.

WICKHAMBREAUX
Off the A257, 5 miles (8 kilometres) east of Canterbury.

LANCASHIRE

Annual events in the county include rushbearing, an egg-rolling competition at Easter and a pram race on Boxing Day. The Medieval Tower House in Turton is open to the public. Tel: (01204) 852203.

North West Tourist Board, Swan House, Swan Meadow Road, Wigan Pier, Wigan, Lancs WN3 5BB. Tel: (01942) 821222.

TURTON
Off the A676, 5 miles (8 kilometres) northwest of Bolton.

WHALLEY
On the B6246, between the A666 and the A671, 3 miles (5 kilometres) south of Clitheroe.

NORFOLK

Annual events in the county include fêtes and flower festivals, as well as country fairs highlighting traditional local crafts.

Norwich Tourist Information Centre, The Guildhall, Norwich. Tel: (01603) 666071.

BLAKENEY
On the A149, 6 miles (10 kilometres) east of Wells-next-the-Sea.

CLEY NEXT THE SEA
Off the A149, 7 miles (11½ kilometres) east of Wells-next-the-Sea.

NEW BUCKENHAM
On the B1113, 14 miles (23 kilometres) south of Norwich.

NORTHAMPTONSHIRE

Annual events in the county include village fairs and garden openings as well as bonfire celebrations.

Northampton Tourist Information Centre, Mr Grant's House, St Giles Square, Northampton NN1 1DA. Tel: (01604) 622677.

GREAT BRINGTON
Off the A428, 6 miles (10 kilometres) northwest of Northampton.

NORTH YORKSHIRE

Annual events in the county include 'Polling the Devil's Knell', a bell-ringing ceremony held every December and the World Coal Carrying Championship in Osset, held every April.

Yorkshire Tourist Board, 312 Tadcaster Road, York YO2 2HF. Tel: (01904) 707961.

BAINBRIDGE
On the A684, in the Pennines, 26 miles (42 kilometres) east of Kendal.

CARLTON-IN-CLEVELAND
Off the A172, 8 miles (13 kilometres) south of Great Ayton.

HUSTHWAITE
Off the A170 and A19, 7 miles (11 kilometres) southeast of Thirsk.

HUTTON-LE-HOLE
Off the A170, 24 miles (39 kilometres) west of Scarborough.

LASTINGHAM
Off the A170, 24 miles (39 kilometres) west of Scarborough.

RIPLEY
On the A61, 4 miles (6 kilometres) north of Harrogate.

STAITHES
Off the A174, 23 miles (37 kilometres) north of Whitby.

WEST TANFIELD
On the A6108, 6 miles (10 kilometres) northwest of Ripon.

NOTTINGHAMSHIRE

Annual events in the county include village fairs and maypole dancing. In late December, farmers in Laxton appoint their Court Leet jury to monitor the open field farming system. Laxton Visitors Centre: Tel: (01777) 871586.

Nottingham Tourist Information, 1–4 Smithy Row, Nottingham N31 2BY. Tel: (0115) 9155330

LAXTON
Between the A1 and the A606, 11 miles (18 kilometres) northeast of Newark-On-Trent.

OXFORDSHIRE

Annual village events include garden open days and village fêtes.

Oxford Tourist Information Centre, The Old School, Gloucester Green, Oxford OX1 2DA. Tel: (01865) 726871.

GREAT TEW
On the B4022, 5 miles (8 kilometres)
northwest of Chipping Norton.

KELMSCOTT
Between the A4095 and the A417,
2 miles (3 kilometres) east of
Lechlade.

SHROPSHIRE

Annual events in the county include
a coracle regatta and raft race in
Ironbridge, as well as fairs and
sporting events.

Telford Tourist Information Centre,
The Management Suite, Telford
Shopping Centre, Telford TF3 4BX.
Tel: (01952) 238008.

TONG
Off the A41, near Junction 3 of the
M54, 6 miles (10 kilometres) east of
Telford.

SOMERSET

Annual events in the county include
farming displays, dances and Punky
Night, a candlelit parade in October.

Yeovil Tourist Information, Petter's
House, Petter's Way, Yeovil BA20 1SH.
Tel: (01935) 471279.

ALLERFORD
On the A39, 5 miles (8 kilometres)
west of Minehead.

CHEWTON MENDIP
On the A39, 6 miles (10 kilometres)
northeast of Wells.

EAST QUANTOXHEAD
Off the A39, 12 miles (20 kilometres)
east along the coast from Minehead.

LUCCOMBE
Off the A39, 3 miles (5 kilometres)
west of Minehead.

PORLOCK WEIR
On the A39, 6 miles (10 kilometres)
west of Minehead.

SELWORTHY
Off the A39, 2 miles (3 kilometres)
west of Minehead.

STAFFORDSHIRE

Annual events in the county include
the Abbots Bromley horn dance, every
September and well dressing in
Longnor and other villages.

Staffordshire Tourism, Development
Services Department, Riverway,
Stafford ST16 3TJ.
Tel: (01785) 277397.

ABBOTS BROMLEY
Off the A515, 6 miles (10 kilometres)
south of Uttoxeter.

LONGNOR
On the B5053, 5 miles (8 kilometres)
south of Buxton.

SUFFOLK

Annual events in the county include
a festival held in Woolpit in late June.
The Aldeburgh Festival of Music is
held in the same month in the village
of Snape.

Ipswich Tourist Information Centre,
St Stephen's Church, St Stephen's
Lane, Ipswich IP1 1DP.
Tel: (01473) 258070.

CLARE
On the A1092, 7 miles (11 kilometres)
east of Haverhill.

HORRINGER
On the A143, 1½ miles
(2½ kilometres) southwest of Bury St
Edmonds.

KERSEY
Off the A1141, 13 miles
(21 kilometres) west of Ipswich.

LAVENHAM
On the A1141, 13 miles
(21 kilometres) southeast of Bury St
Edmonds.

MONKS ELEIGH
On the A1141 and B1115, 5 miles
(8 kilometres) northwest of Hadleigh.

WOOLPIT
On the A45, 8 miles (13 kilometres)
east of Bury St Edmonds.

SURREY

Annual events in the county include
traditional May Day celebrations,
including maypole and morris
dancing.

Guildford Tourist Information Centre,
14 Tunsgate, Guildford GU1 3QT.
Tel: (01483) 444333.

ABINGER COMMON
Off the A25, 4 miles (6 kilometres)
southwest of Dorking.

ABINGER HAMMER
Off the A25, 4 miles (6 kilometres)
west of Dorking.

ALBURY
Off the A248, 3 miles (5 kilometres)
southeast of Guildford.

BLETCHINGLEY
On the A25, 3 miles (5 kilometres)
east of Redhill.

CHIDDINGFOLD
On the A283, 4½ miles
(7 kilometres) northeast of Haslemere.

FRIDAY STREET
Between the A27 and A259, 2 miles
(3 kilometres) north of Eastbourne.

OCKHAM
On the B2039, 1 mile
(1½ kilometres) northwest of East
Horsley and 1½ miles (2 kilometres)
south of Junction 10 of the M25.

SHERE
On the A25, 6 miles (10 kilometres)
west of Dorking.

WITLEY
On the A283, 3 miles (5 kilometres)
south of Godalming.

WEST SUSSEX

Annual events in the county include
displays of fruit and vegetables, garden
open days and the Arundel Festival
towards the end of August, which
includes events such as pea rolling.

West Sussex Tourism, 12 Steyne,
Worthing, West Sussex BN11 3DU.
Tel: (01903) 820667.

AMBERLEY
On the B1239, 5 miles (8 kilometres)
north of Arundel.

BOSHAM
Off the A259, 4 miles
(6½ kilometres) west of Chichester.

WEST YORKSHIRE

Annual events in the county include
rushbearing. Places to visit include the
Brontë Parsonage Museum, Church
Street, Haworth, Keighley, W. Yorks.
Tel: (01535) 642323.

Yorkshire Tourist Board, 312 Tadcaster
Road, York YO2 2HF.
Tel: (01904) 707961.

HAWORTH
On the A6033, 8 miles (13 kilometres)
northwest of Bradford.

WILTSHIRE

Annual events include a regular
programme of fêtes, flower shows and
garden openings, as well as the North
Wiltshire Festival every July.

Salisbury Tourist Information Centre,
Fish Row, Salisbury SP1 9EJ.
Tel: (01722) 334956.

CASTLE COMBE
Off the A350, 5 miles (8 kilometres)
northwest of Chippenham.

INDEX

Abbots Bromley (Staffs.) 80–1
Abinger Common (Surrey) 155
Abinger Hammer (Surrey) 88–9, 182–3
Acland III, Thomas Dyke 18, 136
agriculture 6, 7, 8, 10–13, 23, 28, 191
    dairy farming 178
    fishermen farmers 202
    labour force 75, 79, 163
    land reclamation 164, 188
    water meadows 127
Albury (Surrey) 65
ale 9–10
Alfred, King 154
Alfriston (E.Sussex) 118–19, 138–41
Allerford (Somerset) 136–7
almshouses 89, 166
alum extraction 23
Amberley (W.Sussex) 28–9
anchorites/anchoresses 122
apprenticeships 160
archery 73
Art Nouveau 150
artists' haunts 42, 203
Arts and Crafts Movement 34
Arun, River (Sussex) 28
ashlar construction 39, 59
Austen, Jane 31
Avon, River (Wilts.) 131

Bainbridge (N.Yorks.) 60–1, 156–7
barley 60
barns 18, 60
Battle Abbey (E.Sussex) 139
Bayeux Tapestry 195
beacons 82
beating the bounds 75, 80
beer 9–10
beggars 12
bells, church 96
    bellcotes 111
Berkeley, Vale of 135
Bernard, Sir Francis 121
Bibury (Glos.) 9, 132–3, 172–5
bird sanctuaries 196
Bisley (Glos.) 30–1, 110, 153
Black Death 11, 73
blacksmiths 9, 92, 160–1
Blakeney (Norfolk) 68, 164, 191, 196–7
Bletchingley (Surrey) 81
boats 124–5, 148, 164, 189, 200
    Dunkirk evacuation 206
    narrow boats 158
    shipwrecks 191
    trawlers 204
Bodmin Moor 70
Bolton (Lancs.) 181
bonfire night 75, 92
Bosham (W.Sussex) 10, 190, 194–5
Bradshaw, River (Lancs.) 181
brasses, church 164
Brent Tor (Devon) 108–9

Brett, River (Suffolk) 171
brick 7, 40, 162
    Bosham, W.Sussex 195
    Frampton on Severn, Glos. 57, 135
    Hambleden, Bucks. 99
    Ockham, Surrey 64
    mentioned 68, 82, 86
brick fields 162
bridges 96, 125
    Allerford, Somerset 136
    Bibury, Glos. 132
    Calder Valley viaducts, Lancs. 143
    Castle Combe, Wilts. 131
    Chewton Mendip, Somerset 154
    Eastleach, Glos. 131
    Lower Slaughter, Glos. 147, 148
    Postbridge, Devon 132
    West Tanfield, N.Yorks. 152
Broadway (Herefs. and Worcs.) 42–3
Brontë sisters 69, 116
Bronze Age settlement 23
building materials 26, 28, 38–71,
    161–2, 188
    bridge 132
    church 96–7
burial 96
Burroughs, Steven Barnabas 164
butter crosses 80
butts 73
Byland Abbey (N.Yorks.) 82

Caldbeck (Cumbria) 142
Calder, River (Lancs.) 143
Caldew, River (Cumbria) 142
canals 38, 51, 124, 125, 127, 135, 158,
    163
Canterbury 86
Canute, King 195
Cardigan, Lord (James Thomas
    Brudenell) 99
Carlton-in-Cleveland (N.Yorks.) 23
Carpenter, Christine 122
carpenters' marks 39
cast iron 70, 84
Castle Combe (Wilts.) 130–1
castles 26, 28, 87, 145, 187
cattle see livestock
Cedd, Saint 25
Chalford (Glos.) 51
chancels 95, 96, 119
charcoal 161, 162
Chawton (Hants.) 31
cheese-making 178
Chesil Beach 191
Chetham, Humphrey 181
Chewton Mendip (Somerset) 154–5,
    184–5
Chichester, bishops of 28
Chiddingfold (Surrey) 92–3, 187
Chiltern Hills 99
china clay 70

choir stalls, carved 113, 119
Christleton (Ches.) 89, 158–9
church ales 96
churches 94–7, 184
    Alfriston, E.Sussex 139
    Bisley, Glos. 110
    Bosham, W.Sussex 10, 195
    Brent Tor, Devon 109
    Carlton-in-Cleveland, N.Yorks. 23
    Castle Combe, Wilts. 131
    Chiddingfold, Surrey 187
    Culbone, Somerset 208
    East Quantoxhead, Somerset 26
    Hambleden, Bucks. 98–9, 100
    Hartington, Derbys. 59
    Husthwaite, N.Yorks. 82
    Ivychurch, Kent 121
    Kelmscott, Oxon. 111
    Lavenham, Suffolk 176–7
    Laxton, Notts. 105
    Luxulyan, Cornwall 68, 70
    Much Hadham, Herts. 102
    Nether Winchendon, Bucks. 121
    Romaldkirk, Co.Durham 91
    Selworthy, Somerset 18
    Shere, Surrey 122
    Smarden, Kent 45
    Stoke, Devon 116
    Thaxted, Essex 166
    Tong, Shropshire 112–13
    Weobley, Herefs. and Worcs. 100
    West Tanfield, N.Yorks. 119, 128
    Whalley, Lancs. 53
    Wickhambreaux, Kent 150
    Woolpit, Suffolk 107
    mentioned 25, 63, 65, 84, 116, 135, 145,
        164, 169, 171, 174, 196, 198
churchwardens 12, 95–6
Civil War 85, 107
clapper bridges 125, 131, 132
Clare (Suffolk) 62–3
clay in construction 40–1, 162
Cleveland Hills 23
Cley next the Sea (Norfolk) 164–5
Clifford, Rosamond 135
clocks 100, 183
cloth trade see textile trades
Clovelly (Devon) 198–9
Clutterbuck, Richard 135
coastal villages 188–91
    Blakeney, Norfolk 191, 196
    Bosham, W.Sussex 190, 195
    Cley next the Sea, Norfolk 164
    Clovelly, Devon 198
    Lynmouth, Devon 206
    Polperro, Cornwall 200–3, 206
    Porlock Weir, Somerset 208
    Portloe, Cornwall 192
    Staithes, N.Yorks 204
cob 26, 40, 41
Coleridge, Samuel Taylor 206

Coln, River (Glos.) 132, 172
colour
    in churches 100, 113, 117
    colour wash 26, 78, 202
common land 9, 11, 12, 72
commuters 13
consecrated ground 96
Cook, Captain James 189
copper mines 162
Cornish granite 68, 70
Cotswolds 39, 42, 51, 66, 97, 132, 145,
    172
cottage industries 160, 162–3
cotton industry 181
crafts 160–3
cricket 89
Crimean War 99
Cromwell, Oliver 85
crop rotation 10–11
Crosby Garrett (Cumbria) 63
crosses, medieval 66, 73, 80, 85, 143
cruck construction 38, 57
Crystal Palace, Hyde Park 169
Cuckmere, River (E.Sussex) 139, 141
customs and excise 200
cutlery industry 166

dairy farming 178
Danish raids 25
Dartmoor 79, 109, 115, 132
de Clare family 81, 166
de Pembruge, Elizabeth 113
de Vere, John (13th Earl of Oxford) 177
Dee, River (Cheshire) 158
Derby, Earl of 169
Derbyshire well dressing 153
Diana, Princess of Wales 13
Dissolution of the Monasteries 12, 36,
    143
Dr Dolittle (film) 131
Domesday Book 8, 81, 150, 172
domestic servants 74
doors 39, 50
    door mouldings 105, 174
Douglas, John 89
Dove, River (Peak District) 59, 178
Dover (Kent) 191
Dowsing, William 107
drinking fountains 84
drystone walling see walls
Dufton (Cumbria) 90
Dunster Castle (Somerset) 26

earth walls see walls
East Anglia 41, 97, 107, 181
East Dart River (Devon) 132
East Quantoxhead (Somerset) 26–7
Eastleach Martin/Turville (Glos.) 131
Eaton Hall (Cheshire) 89
Edward III, King 44, 85, 162
Edward VI, King 92

eels 125
effigies *see* monuments, church
Elizabeth I, Queen 30, 191
enclosures 11, 12, 60
English Heritage 82, 90, 143
erosion, coastal 188
Ethelbert, King 95
Evelyn, William John 155
Exmoor National Park 18, 208
Eye, River (Glos.) 147

factories 163
fairs 73–4, 79, 92
Falkland, Lord 46
farming *see* agriculture
farriers 160–1
Fastolf, Sir John 131
Fawkes, Guy 75, 92
ferries 125
festivals 74–5
feudal system 8, 11
field boundaries 8, 60
Finchingfield (Essex) 168
fish/fishing 125, 127, 188, 190–1, 192,
    198, 202, 204
flash locks 126
flint 40
    Alfriston, E.Sussex 119
    Blakeney, Norfolk 68
    Hambleden, Bucks. 99
    Much Hadham, Herts. 102
    mentioned 86
floods 95, 127, 204, 206
fords 125, 136
foresters 157
forests 7, 161–2
forges 162
Forster, E.M. 89
Frampton on Severn (Glos.) 56–7,
    134–5
Friday Street (Surrey) 183
fulling mills 132, 162

Gallantin, Count James 150
gardens 12, 36–7, 78
gargoyles 105
geology and scenery 6, 188
Georgian England 64, 70, 102, 107, 135,
    174, 198
Giffard, Robert 109
gilding 100
glass 53, 161, 184, 203
    glassmakers 187
    stained-glass 97
Glaven, River (Norfolk) 164
glebe lands 95
Gloucester and Sharpness Canal 135
glovemakers 162
goldsmiths 166
grain exports/imports 12, 196
granite 68, 70, 115, 202
Graves, John Woodcock 142
graves/gravestones 45, 96
Great Brington (Northants.) 13
Great Dun Fell (Cumbria) 87
Great Exhibition (1851) 169

Great Tew (Oxon.) 46–7
greens, village 9, 72–5
    Abinger Hammer, Surrey 89
    Alfriston, E.Sussex 119
    Bainbridge, N.Yorks. 157
    Chiddingfold, Surrey 92
    Christleton, Cheshire 89
    Dufton, Cumbria 90
    Frampton on Severn, Glos. 135
    Hambleden, Bucks. 99
    Husthwaite, N.Yorks. 82–3
    Hutton-le-Hole, N.Yorks. 126
    Milburn, Cumbria 87
    Monks Eleigh, Suffolk 84
    New Buckenham, Norfolk 73
    Selborne, Hants. 16
    Selworthy, Somerset 18
    Wickhambreaux, Kent 86
gritstone *see* millstone grit
grotesques 105
guilds 163
    guildhalls 78, 166
gunpowder 162

Hadrian's Wall 90
Halloween 75
Hambleden (Bucks.) 99, 100
Hambledon Hills (N.Yorks.) 82
Hamlyn, Christine 198
hammer ponds 183
hammerbeam roofs 107
Harold, King 195
Hartington (Derbys.) 58–9
harvest home 75
Hastings, Battle of 39, 195
Haworth (W.Yorks.) 69, 116
Henry II, King 86, 116, 135
Henry VII, King 102
Henry VIII, King 30, 97, 99, 116,
    191
herbal medicine 36
hiring fairs 74
holiday resorts 206
holy wells 153
Horn Dance (Abbots Bromley, Staffs.)
    80
    see also morris men
Horringer (Suffolk) 54–5
horse power 127, 158, 160–1
horse-racing 132
house-numbering 21
Howgill Castle (Cumbria) 87
hunter-gatherers 7
hunting 142
Husthwaite (N.Yorks.) 82–3
Hutton-le-Hole (N.Yorks.) 126

Ice Ages 7, 147, 157
Industrial Revolution 6, 127, 163, 181,
    183
Ingilby family (Ripley, N.Yorks.) 85
inns *see* public houses
iron 84, 162, 183
    ironwork 70
Isle of Wight 94
Ivychurch (Kent) 120–1

jails 72
jet stone 23, 204
Johnson, Ben 46

kaolin 70
Keble, John 131
Keble, Thomas 110, 153
Kelmscott (Oxon.) 32–5, 111
Kersey (Suffolk) 170–1
Kingsley, Charles 198
kissing gates 122

labour 11, 12–13, 51, 74, 75, 148, 160–3
lace-workers 162–3
Lake District National Park 142
land reclamation 164, 188
landowners 8, 11, 65, 95, 125, 127, 148,
    161
Lastingham (N.Yorks.) 25
Lavenham (Suffolk) 48–9, 76–8, 176–7
Laxton (Notts.) 104–5
Leach, River (Glos.) 131
lead mining 184
legends *see* myths and legends
lifeboat services 191, 204
lighthouses 191
limestone 39, 46, 49, 59, 60, 68
limewash 41, 49
Lincolnshire 39
livestock 9, 11, 12, 23, 73
    fairs 74, 79
    husbandry 60, 84, 87, 178
    see also wool trade
lock-ups 72, 78
locks, canal 126–7, 158
Longnor (Staffs.) 178–9
Louden, John Claudius 46
Lower Slaughter (Glos.) 147–9
Luccombe (Somerset) 26
Luttrell family (E.Quantoxhead) 26
Lutyens, Sir Edwin 122, 145
Luxulyan (Cornwall) 68, 70
lych gates 99, 122
Lynmouth (Devon) 206

Manchester, Chetham Library in 181
manorial system 8, 11, 35, 73, 95, 157,
    161
mantraps 12
market crosses 73, 85
markets 73, 76, 81, 92
Marmion, Sir John 128
Marston Moor, Battle of 85
mathematical tiles 40, 64
May Day festival 75
maypoles 75
mechanisation 12–13
Mendip Hills 184
metals 162
Milburn (Cumbria) 87
millers 161, 164, 168
mills *see* water power
millstone grit 40, 59
    Haworth, W.Yorks. 69
    Longnor, Staffs. 178
mining 23, 59, 66, 79, 162, 184, 204

misericords 119
monasteries 12, 25, 36, 50, 100, 116, 132,
    139, 143
Monks Eleigh (Suffolk) 84
monuments, church 96, 97, 102, 113,
    128, 174
Moore, Henry 102
mop fairs 74
Morland (Cumbria) 125
Morris, William 32–5, 111, 174
morris dancing 72, 75
    see also Horn Dance
mourning jewellery 204
Much Hadham (Herts.) 102–3
myths and legends 30, 63, 105, 115,
    192, 195

Napoleonic Wars 12, 189–90
narrow boats 158
National Trust 18, 26, 141, 172, 192, 196
navigation, maritime 109, 116, 191, 196
navvies 127
Neolithic settlement 7, 147
Nether Winchendon (Bucks.) 121
New Buckenham (Norfolk) 73
Norfolk Broads 125
Norman England 8, 26, 131, 145
North Sea 204
North York Moors National Park
    23, 25, 82

oak
    doors 50
    timber frames 38–9
Oates, Captain Lawrence 16
Ockham (Surrey) 64
Oxford 148
    Oxford Movement 131

packhorse routes 23, 136, 154
painted ceilings 100
pargetting 39, 62–3
parish clerks 95
parish pumps 73, 84, 90
parish registers 94
passing bell 96
paths, coastal 189
Paxton, Joseph 169
Peak District National Park 59, 169, 178
Peel, John 142
Pennines 60, 90, 91, 132
pews, carved 107, 119
Pilgrimage of Grace 50
pilgrims 86
plagues 11, 25, 73
plasterwork 63, 76, 115
Plough Monday 75
Plymouth Sound 109
poaching 12, 125
pollution 69
Polperro (Cornwall) 200–3, 206
ponds 73, 92, 135, 183
poor souls lights 110
population 6, 8, 11, 73, 191
porches 70, 203
    church 107, 117

Porlock (Somerset) 136, 208–9
Portloe (Cornwall) 192–3
post mills 168
Postbridge (Devon) 132
pound locks 126–7
pounds, manorial 9, 73
poverty 12, 51, 110, 116, 166
press-gangs 189–90
priests 95–6
public houses 9–10, 13, 75, 91, 139, 181
Pugin, Augustus 65
pumps, village 73, 84, 90
Puritans 97

Quaker villages 157
quarries 59, 66, 68, 145
quatrefoils 122

ragstone 121
railways 28, 38, 127, 143, 158, 163, 169,
    190–1, 206
Reformation 97
Regency England 70
regional products 160
reservoirs 127
ridgeways, ancient 139
riots 13, 92
Ripley (N.Yorks.) 74, 85
river travel 124–5
roads 21, 96, 124, 125, 152, 154
Rogationtide Festival 75
Romaldkirk (Co.Durham) 91
Roman Britain 7–8, 40, 82, 127, 157,
    172, 184, 188, 191
    Hadrian's Wall 90
Romney Marsh (Kent) 121
rood screens 107, 116
Rosencrantz, Arild 150
Rossetti, Dante Gabriel 32, 35
roundhouses 192
royal charters 73, 74, 92, 191
Royal National Lifeboat Institution 191

Sackville, Sir Thomas 132
St John's Beck (Cumbria) 60–1
St Paul's Cathedral 70
Salvin, Anthony 26
sanctuary, right of 95
sandstone 23, 39–40, 59, 69, 87, 113
Sanger, Reverend George 23
Sankey Canal (Lancs.) 127
Saxon England 8, 23, 60, 107, 184
    burial sites 119, 139
    churches 95, 96, 195
Scots 87
Scott, George Gilbert 107
Scrope family (Castle Combe) 131
seaweed 191
sedilias 119
Selborne (Hants.) 15–17, 36–7
Selworthy (Somerset) 18–19, 136
Semer Water (N.Yorks.) 157
Severn, River 135
sextons 95
sheep 11, 12, 172
Shelley, Percy Bysshe 206

Shere (Surrey) 122–3
shipwrecks 191
shops 13, 21, 42, 161, 186
Shropshire Union Canal 158
signposts 21
silk industry 162, 169
Smarden (Kent) 44–5
Smith, W.H. 99
smuggling 121, 136, 139, 189, 200, 208
socialist movement 34
Society for the Protection of Ancient
    Buildings 32, 141
South Downs 139
Spanish Armada 82
spire finials 105
Spring family (Lavenham) 177
springs 124
squatters' rights 72
squint windows 26, 122
stained-glass 97, 187
Staithes (N.Yorks.) 189, 204–5
standing stones 63
Stanton (Glos.) 66–7
stocks 72, 85, 89, 91
Stodmarsh (Kent) 150
Stoke (Hartland Quay, Devon) 116–17
stone buildings 7, 10, 39–40, 132, 143
    Allerford, Somerset 136
    Bibury, Glos. 172, 174
    Bosham, W.Sussex 10, 195
    Broadway, Herefs. and Worcs.. 42
    Chalford, Glos. 51
    Great Tew, Oxon. 46
    Haworth, W.Yorks. 69
    Ivychurch, Kent 121
    Lavenham, Suffolk 176
    Longnor, Staffs. 178
    Luxulyan, Cornwall 68, 70
    Milburn, Cumbria 87
    Polperro, Cornwall 202
    Romaldkirk, Co.Durham 91
    the Slaughters, Glos. 145, 147
    Stanton, Glos. 66
    Tong, Salop 113
    Widecombe-in-the-Moor, Devon 115
Stott, Sir Philip 66
Stour, River (Kent) 86, 150
Strahan, John 135
sundials 100, 158
supermarkets 13
superstitions see myths and legends

Taylor, Isaac 76
Teesdale 91
Tennyson, Alfred Lord 99
textile trades 12, 97, 162–3
    Gloucestershire 30, 51, 132, 172
    Kent 44
    Lancashire 181
    Suffolk 76, 78, 171, 177
    Wiltshire 131
    Yorkshire 116
Thames, River 32
Thames and Severn Canal 51
thatch 41, 54, 135, 141
Thaxted (Essex) 161, 166–7

three field system 10–11
tiles
    church floor 97, 113
    mathematical 40, 64
    roof 49, 128
    tile cladding 40, 53, 65, 81, 89, 195
Tillingbourne, River (Surrey) 89, 183
timber buildings 7, 38–9, 53, 64, 96,
    161–2
    Alfriston, E.Sussex 139
    Finchingfield, Essex 168
    Husthwaite, N.Yorks. 82
    Kersey, Suffolk 171
    Lavenham, Suffolk 49, 76
    Nether Winchendon, Bucks. 121
    Smarden, Kent 44
    Thaxted, Essex 166
    Weobley, Herefs. and Worcs. 57
    Woolpit, Suffolk 107
    mentioned 135
tin-mining 79
tithes 95
tofts 9
tolls 73, 125, 152, 161
tombs see monuments, church
Tong (Shropshire) 70, 97, 112–13
topiary 54
towers, church 97, 99
trade routes, waterway 124–5, 127, 164,
    189, 196
tradesmen's signs 21
transport 124–6, 136, 143, 148, 152, 154,
    163
Trinity House, Corporation of 191
Tudor, Edmund 102
Tudor England 12, 40, 80, 102, 107, 132
turnpike roads 21, 125, 152
Turton (Lancs.) 39, 89, 180–1
twill weave cloth 171

undertakers 160
Upper Slaughter (Glos.) 41, 144–7
Ure, River (Yorks.) 128, 152, 157

vagabonds 12
Vernon, Sir Richard 97
Veryan Bay, Cornwall 192
viaducts, railway 143
Victorian England 34, 54, 75, 97, 174,
    204, 206
villeins 8

wagon roofs, church 18, 115, 116
Waller, Edmund 46
walls 39
    drystone walling 59, 60
    earth walls 7, 26, 40–1
    wall-paintings 97, 99
war memorials 89
water diviners 155
water meadows 127, 128, 135
water power 51, 125, 126, 132, 161, 162
    Abinger Hammer, Surrey 183
    Bibury, Glos. 172
    Caldbeck, Cumbria 142
    Lower Slaughter, Glos. 148

Wickhambreaux, Kent 150, 163
water supplies 7, 84, 124, 127, 132, 147,
    153
waterways 51, 124–7
wattle and daub 39, 49
Weald 183
    Wealden houses 44
weather-boarding 89, 150, 168
weather-tiling see tiles
weathercocks 105
weavers, see textile trades
Webb, Philip 111
weekenders 13
weirs 125–6
wells 73, 89, 153, 155
Wensleydale 60, 157
Weobley (Herefs. and Worcs.) 57, 100–1
West Tanfield (N.Yorks.) 119, 128–9, 152
Westminster Abbey 187
Whalley (Lancs.) 50, 52–3, 143
wheelwrights 161
wherries 124–5
whipping posts 72, 89
Whitby (N.Yorks.) 204
White, Gilbert 15–17
White Horse (Hambledon Hills,
    N.Yorks.) 82
Wickhambreaux (Kent) 86, 150–1, 163
Widecombe-in-the-Moor (Devon) 79,
    114–15
Wilberforce, Samuel 89
Wildboarclough (Ches.) 169
wildlife 15, 196, 208
William I of England, King (the
    Conqueror) 8, 195
windmills 161, 164, 166, 168
windows 52–3, 64, 184
    squint windows 122
    stained-glass 97, 150, 187
    window mouldings 105, 174
Windrush, River 147, 148
Windsor Castle 187
wishing wells 153
witchcraft 105
Witley (Surrey) 53
Wolsey, Cardinal 99
wolves 107
wooden buildings see timber buildings
woodland crafts 160
wool trade 12, 97, 162
    Cotswold 172
    Devon 132
    Kent 44
    Suffolk 76, 78, 177
    Wiltshire 131
    see also livestock
Woolpit (Suffolk) 106–7
World Heritage Sites 90
World Wars 13, 96, 178, 206
wrack 191